Affirmations for Creativity

Affirmations for creativity

Rosa Maria Aguado

Published by ruby red, 2024.

AFFIRMATIONS FOR CREATIVITY

First edition. April 2, 2024.

Copyright © 2024 Rosa Maria Aguado.

ISBN: 979-8224645893

Written by Rosa Maria Aguado.

We kindly ask that you respect the copyright of this book, 'Affirmations for Creativity' which encompasses all its content, including text, images, and ideas. Permission to reproduce, distribute, or transmit any portion of this publication in any form must be obtained in advance from the author. Exceptions are made for brief quotations used in critical reviews and certain noncommercial uses as permitted by copyright law.

While we've taken great care to ensure the accuracy and completeness of this work, please understand that the author and publisher cannot guarantee its suitability for every reader's needs. The advice and strategies provided may not apply universally.

We sincerely hope that this book enriches your life, but it's important to note that the author and publisher cannot be held responsible for any loss of profit or other damages, whether direct or incidental, resulting from the use of this material. We encourage you to seek professional advice when necessary.

By accessing and using this book, you agree to abide by these terms and conditions. If you disagree, we kindly ask that you refrain from accessing or using this book. We appreciate your understanding and cooperation

Every obstacle is a stepping stone toward unlocking fresh and inventive solutions.

I trust in the dynamic nature of my thoughts, adapting and evolving with creativity.

My mind is an expansive playground where ideas frolic and intertwine.

The landscapes of my imagination are ever-expanding, offering new vistas for exploration.

I trust in the divine flow of creative energy, allowing inspiration to guide my actions.

Every idea is a spark that ignites the flame of innovation within me.

I am a vessel for creative energy, allowing it to flow through me and manifest in beautiful ways.

I celebrate the diversity of my creative expressions, recognizing each as a unique masterpiece.

My mind is a fertile ground for creative seeds to take root and flourish.

I trust the intuitive whispers of inspiration that guide me towards inspired actions.

I celebrate the diversity of my creative expressions, recognizing each as a valuable contribution.

My mind is a workshop of endless possibilities, crafting ideas into tangible expressions.

Every creative endeavor is a collaboration between my thoughts and the universal flow of inspiration.

I embrace the serendipity of creative discovery, finding beauty in the unexpected.

I celebrate the spontaneous dance of inspiration, leading me to groundbreaking discoveries.

Every moment is an opportunity for a fresh and ingenious concept.

My thoughts are a symphony of originality, creating harmonies that resonate with the universe.

Challenges are gateways to inventive problem-solving and creative growth.

I welcome the diversity of thoughts, fostering a rich tapestry of imaginative expressions.

The canvas of my mind is painted with strokes of ingenious brilliance.

I trust the ebb and flow of my creative energy, allowing it to adapt and evolve effortlessly.

In the sanctuary of my mind, creative sparks illuminate the darkness, revealing endless possibilities.

The symphony of my thoughts plays a melody of innovation that reverberates through my actions.

I release any fear of judgment, allowing my creative expressions to flow authentically.

I am a vessel for the universal energy of inspiration, channeling it into my creative pursuits.

My thoughts are like seeds planted in the soil of my mind, growing into flourishing fields of creativity.

The architecture of my mind is built with the bricks of inventive ideas and imaginative designs.

I trust that the universe supports and amplifies my creative endeavors.

I am a conductor orchestrating the harmonious melodies of creative thoughts and ideas.

The currents of creative energy flow through me, connecting me to the infinite reservoir of inspiration.

The kaleidoscope of ideas in my mind forms a rich mosaic of creative possibilities.

The symphony of inspiration orchestrates beautiful melodies in every area of my life.

I welcome the unexpected twists and turns of my creative path, trusting they lead to new opportunities.

Challenges are mere gateways to innovative solutions, and I navigate through them with ease.

The fertile ground of my thoughts nurtures seeds of creativity that blossom into unique expressions.

Challenges are mere stepping stones, guiding me towards unexplored realms of inventive solutions.

Every idea is a journey, and I embark on these creative adventures with enthusiasm and curiosity.

The landscapes of my imagination are ever-expanding, offering new vistas for exploration.

The alchemy of my mind transforms ordinary thoughts into extraordinary and innovative concepts.

My creative intuition is a guiding star, leading me towards uncharted territories of inspiration.

My mind is an open channel, inviting winds of inspiration to carry in new and novel concepts.

I embrace the cyclical nature of inventiveness, honoring periods of rest and reflection.

Challenges are opportunities for inventive problem-solving and creative evolution.

The architecture of my thoughts is built with the bricks of inventive ideas and original designs.

My mind is an open gateway for inspiration, inviting inventive ideas to flow freely.

The seeds of innovation planted in my thoughts germinate into flourishing fields of creativity.

I celebrate the dance of ideas in my mind, a choreography of inventive concepts.

The river of inspiration flows gracefully through me, carving new pathways and shaping my destiny.

Challenges are mere stepping stones, guiding me towards innovative solutions and growth.

I trust the serendipity of inventive discovery, finding beauty in the unexpected.

Every obstacle is an opportunity for my inventive nature to showcase resilience and resourcefulness.

The symphony of creativity orchestrates beautiful melodies in every area of my life.

I release any fear of judgment, allowing my inventive expressions to radiate with authenticity.

I am a vessel for the universal flow of inventive energy, shaping my reality with flair.

My mind is a fertile ground where seeds of innovation sprout into groundbreaking concepts.

I embrace the dance of creativity, letting it guide me to new and unexplored territories.

Innovative solutions reveal themselves effortlessly, like stars illuminating the night sky.

Challenges are invitations for my inventive spirit to shine brightly and find ingenious answers.

Every thought carries the potential to birth a novel idea, contributing to the tapestry of innovation.

The symphony of my thoughts resonates with the harmonious chords of originality.

I am a conduit for inventive energy, channeling it into every aspect of my life.

The landscape of my mind is an ever-evolving canvas painted with strokes of ingenious ideas.

In the playground of my imagination, I joyfully explore the infinite realms of inventiveness.

I welcome the unpredictable nature of creative exploration, finding joy in the unexpected.

The canvas of my mind is painted with strokes of inventive brilliance, creating a vibrant masterpiece.

I welcome the chaos of creative exploration, knowing that within it lies the seeds of innovation.

My thoughts are seeds of potential, germinating into lush forests of inventive concepts.

I trust the serendipity of inventive discovery, finding beauty in the unexpected.

I am a magnet for inspiration, attracting inventive ideas effortlessly and naturally.

The symphony of creativity orchestrates beautiful melodies in every area of my life.

I release any fear of judgment, allowing my inventive expressions to radiate with authenticity.

I am a vessel for the universal flow of inventive energy, shaping my reality with flair.

My mind is a boundless canvas, ready to capture the brushstrokes of inspired thoughts.

The fountain of inventive ideas within me is boundless and ever-flowing.

I trust the serendipity of inventive discovery, finding beauty in the unexpected.

I am a magnet for inspiration, attracting inventive ideas effortlessly and naturally.

The symphony of creativity orchestrates beautiful melodies in every area of my life.

I release any fear of judgment, allowing my inventive expressions to radiate with authenticity.

I am a vessel for the universal flow of inventive energy, shaping my reality with flair.

Every creative endeavor is a tapestry woven with threads of innovation and ingenuity.

I celebrate the dance of ideas in my mind, a choreography of inventive thoughts.

The wellspring of inventive energy within me is eternal, continually refreshing with new and imaginative ideas.

I trust in the infinite intelligence of my inventive mind, guiding me towards unique expressions.

I am an artist of thoughts, sculpting ideas into tangible and impactful forms.

I release any self-imposed limitations, allowing my inventive thoughts to soar to new heights.

The river of inspiration flows through me, carving new pathways and shaping my destiny.

Every creative endeavor is a tapestry woven with threads of innovation and ingenuity.

I celebrate the dance of ideas in my mind, a choreography of inventive thoughts.

The wellspring of inventive energy within me is eternal, continually refreshing with new and imaginative ideas.

I trust in the infinite intelligence of my inventive mind, guiding me towards unique expressions.

I am an artist of thoughts, sculpting ideas into tangible and impactful forms.

The canvas of my mind is painted with strokes of inventive brilliance, creating a vibrant masterpiece.

I welcome the chaos of creative exploration, knowing that within it lies the seeds of innovation.

My thoughts are seeds of potential, germinating into lush forests of inventive concepts.

I release any self-imposed limitations, allowing my inventive thoughts to soar to new heights.

The river of inspiration flows through me, carving new pathways and shaping my destiny.

Every creative endeavor is a tapestry woven with threads of innovation and ingenuity.

I celebrate the dance of ideas in my mind, a choreography of inventive thoughts.

The wellspring of inventive energy within me is eternal, continually refreshing with new and imaginative ideas.

I trust in the infinite intelligence of my inventive mind, guiding me towards unique expressions.

I am an artist of thoughts, sculpting ideas into tangible and impactful forms.

The canvas of my mind is painted with strokes of inventive brilliance, creating a vibrant masterpiece.

I welcome the chaos of creative exploration, knowing that within it lies the seeds of innovation.

My thoughts are seeds of potential, germinating into lush forests of inventive concepts.

I am an artist of thoughts, sculpting ideas into tangible and impactful forms.

The canvas of my mind is painted with strokes of inventive brilliance, creating a vibrant masterpiece.

I welcome the chaos of creative exploration, knowing that within it lies the seeds of innovation.

My thoughts are seeds of potential, germinating into lush forests of inventive concepts.

I trust the serendipity of inventive discovery, finding beauty in the unexpected.

I am a magnet for inspiration, attracting inventive ideas effortlessly and naturally.

The symphony of creativity orchestrates beautiful melodies in every area of my life.

I release any fear of judgment, allowing my inventive expressions to radiate with authenticity.

I am a vessel for the universal flow of inventive energy, shaping my reality with flair.

My mind is a boundless canvas, ready to capture the brushstrokes of inspired thoughts.

The symphony of creativity orchestrates beautiful melodies in every area of my life.

I release any fear of judgment, allowing my inventive expressions to radiate with authenticity.

I am a vessel for the universal flow of inventive energy, shaping my reality with flair.

My mind is a boundless canvas, ready to capture the brushstrokes of inspired thoughts.

I release any self-imposed limitations, allowing my inventive thoughts to soar to new heights.

The river of inspiration flows through me, carving new pathways and shaping my destiny.

Every creative endeavor is a tapestry woven with threads of innovation and ingenuity.

I celebrate the dance of ideas in my mind, a choreography of inventive thoughts.

The wellspring of inventive energy within me is eternal, continually refreshing with new and imaginative ideas.

I trust in the infinite intelligence of my inventive mind, guiding me towards unique expressions.

My creative essence is a guiding force, fueling my journey towards new horizons.

I trust the serendipity of inventive discovery, finding beauty in the unexpected.

I am a magnet for inspiration, attracting inventive ideas effortlessly and naturally.

The symphony of creativity orchestrates beautiful melodies in every area of my life.

I release any fear of judgment, allowing my inventive expressions to radiate with authenticity.

I am a vessel for the universal flow of inventive energy, shaping my reality with flair.

My mind is a boundless canvas, ready to capture the brushstrokes of inspired thoughts.

I release any self-imposed limitations, allowing my inventive thoughts to soar to new heights.

I trust the serendipity of inventive discovery, finding beauty in the unexpected.

I am a magnet for inspiration, attracting inventive ideas effortlessly and naturally.

I am a conduit for the universal flow of creative energy, channeling inspiration into my endeavors.

The tapestry of my thoughts is woven with threads of imaginative brilliance and ingenuity.

I release any fear of judgment and allow my creative expressions to flow authentically.

I am a vessel for the magic of inventive inspiration, and it flows through me effortlessly.

Challenges are opportunities for my inventive nature to shine.

The playground of my thoughts is a breeding ground for originality and creativity.

I welcome the unfolding of my imaginative potential in every moment.

Challenges are stepping stones, guiding me toward ingenious breakthroughs.

The tapestry of my ideas weaves together a rich mosaic of inventive possibilities.

I trust in the spontaneous dance of my thoughts, leading to innovative insights.

I trust the process of creative evolution, embracing each stage with openness and curiosity.

I am a conduit for the universal flow of creative energy, channeling inspiration into my endeavors.

The tapestry of my thoughts is woven with threads of imaginative brilliance and ingenuity.

I release any fear of judgment and allow my creative expressions to flow authentically.

I am a vessel for the magic of inventive inspiration, and it flows through me effortlessly.

My creative spirit is resilient, overcoming challenges with inventive solutions.

Every moment is an opportunity for creative expression and artistic exploration.

I am an architect of inventive ideas, constructing a reality that reflects my imaginative vision.

My mind is a fertile ground where ideas germinate, grow, and blossom into innovative concepts.

I trust the process of creative evolution, embracing each stage with openness and curiosity.

I embrace the beauty of uncertainty, knowing it often leads to profound moments of inspiration.

My mind is a sanctuary for innovative thoughts, where ideas bloom and flourish.

I welcome the flow of inventive energy, allowing it to inspire and uplift me.

I am open to creative breakthroughs that lead to new and exciting possibilities.

Challenges are invitations to tap into the well of inventive inspiration within me.

Every idea I conceive is a spark that ignites the flame of innovation within my soul.

My creative essence is resilient, overcoming challenges with inventive solutions.

Every moment is an opportunity for creative expression and artistic exploration.

I am an architect of inventive ideas, constructing a reality that reflects my imaginative vision.

My mind is a fertile ground where ideas germinate, grow, and blossom into innovative concepts.

The symphony of my inventive mind resonates with the harmonious frequencies of creativity.

I release any resistance to change, embracing inspiration that guides me to brilliance.

I am open to receiving inventive insights from unexpected sources and unlikely places.

The river of creative energy flows through me, carrying with it the seeds of new ideas.

Challenges serve as invitations to explore uncharted realms of inventive thinking.

Every idea I conceive is a stepping stone toward greater creativity and innovation.

My mind is a fertile ground for creative seeds to take root and flourish.

I trust the intuitive whispers of inventive inspiration that guide me toward inspired actions.

Challenges are opportunities for creative exploration and ingenious problem-solving.

The canvas of my life is painted with strokes of inventive brilliance and originality.

My thoughts are seeds of potential, germinating into lush forests of inventive concepts.

My mind is a wellspring of creative ideas and innovative solutions.

I effortlessly tap into my creative reservoir to generate inventive concepts.

Every challenge is an opportunity for my inventive nature to shine.

The playground of my thoughts is a breeding ground for originality and creativity.

I welcome the unfolding of my imaginative potential in every moment.

Challenges are stepping stones, guiding me toward ingenious breakthroughs.

The tapestry of my ideas weaves together a rich mosaic of inventive possibilities.

I trust in the spontaneous dance of my thoughts, leading to innovative insights.

My creative essence is a guiding force, fueling my journey towards new horizons.

The symphony of creativity resonates within me, guiding me towards inventive and ingenious solutions.

I welcome the unknown with excitement, trusting that creativity will illuminate the path ahead.

Every challenge is an opportunity for innovative problem-solving and creative growth.

I celebrate the dance of ideas in my mind, a choreography of inventive thoughts.

The wellspring of inventive energy within me is eternal, continually refreshing with new and imaginative ideas.

I trust in the infinite intelligence of my inventive mind, guiding me towards unique expressions.

I am an artist of thoughts, sculpting ideas into tangible and impactful forms.

The canvas of my mind is painted with strokes of inventive brilliance, creating a vibrant masterpiece.

I welcome the chaos of creative exploration, knowing that within it lies the seeds of innovation.

My thoughts are seeds of potential, germinating into lush forests of inventive concepts.

I release any fear of judgment, allowing my inventive expressions to shine authentically.

I am a vessel for the universal flow of inventive energy, shaping my reality with flair.

My mind is an open channel, inviting winds of inspiration to carry in new and novel concepts.

I embrace the cyclical nature of creativity, honoring periods of rest and reflection.

Challenges are mere stepping stones to innovative solutions and creative evolution.

The architecture of my thoughts is built with the bricks of inventive ideas and original designs.

I celebrate the kaleidoscope of ideas, recognizing each as a valuable contribution to my creativity.

My mind is a workshop where thoughts are sculpted into tangible expressions of ingenuity.

Every creative endeavor is a collaboration between my thoughts and the universal flow of inspiration.

I trust in the synchronicity of my inventive thoughts, leading me towards inspired actions.

I am an artist of thoughts, sculpting ideas into tangible and impactful forms.

The canvas of my mind is painted with strokes of inventive brilliance, creating a vibrant masterpiece.

I welcome the chaos of creative exploration, knowing that within it lies the seeds of innovation.

The essence of my thoughts is transformative, shaping my surroundings with inventive energy.

In my mental workshop, ideas are crafted into tangible expressions of ingenuity.

The symphony of my thoughts plays melodies that reverberate with inventive inspiration.

I am a conductor of innovative ideas, orchestrating a harmonious flow in my mind.

I welcome the dynamic interplay of ideas, blending them into a mosaic of creativity.

Every idea is a brushstroke painting the canvas of my mind with vibrant and imaginative hues.

I trust that the universe supports and amplifies my creative thought processes.

The symphony of creativity orchestrates beautiful melodies in every area of my life.

I release any fear of judgment, allowing my inventive expressions to radiate with authenticity.

I am a vessel for the universal flow of inventive energy, shaping my reality with flair.

My mind is a boundless canvas, ready to capture the brushstrokes of inspired thoughts.

I release any self-imposed limitations, allowing my inventive thoughts to soar to new heights.

The river of inspiration flows through me, carving new pathways and shaping my destiny.

Every creative endeavor is a tapestry woven with threads of innovation and ingenuity.

I celebrate the dance of ideas in my mind, a choreography of inventive thoughts.

The wellspring of inventive energy within me is eternal, continually refreshing with new and imaginative ideas.

I trust in the infinite intelligence of my inventive mind, guiding me toward unique expressions.

The symphony of my thoughts creates a melody of inspiration that echoes in my actions.

Challenges are gateways to creative solutions, and I navigate them with inventive flair.

The landscapes of my imagination continually evolve, offering new realms for exploration.

I release any limitations, allowing my thoughts to soar into innovative heights.

I celebrate the spontaneous dance of ideas in my mind, a ballet of inventiveness.

The river of inspiration flows gracefully through me, carving pathways of creative expression.

Every challenge is an opportunity to showcase my inventive and resourceful nature.

I trust in the serendipity of creative discovery, finding beauty in the unexpected.

I trust the serendipity of inventive discovery, finding beauty in the unexpected.

I am a magnet for inspiration, attracting inventive ideas effortlessly and naturally.

I am a magnet for inspiration, attracting inventive ideas effortlessly and naturally.

The symphony of creativity orchestrates beautiful melodies in every area of my life.

I release any fear of judgment, allowing my inventive expressions to radiate with authenticity.

I am a vessel for the universal flow of inventive energy, shaping my reality with flair.

My mind is a boundless canvas, ready to capture the brushstrokes of inspired thoughts.

I release any self-imposed limitations, allowing my inventive thoughts to soar to new heights.

The river of inspiration flows through me, carving new pathways and shaping my destiny.

Every creative endeavor is a tapestry woven with threads of innovation and ingenuity.

I celebrate the dance of ideas in my mind, a choreography of inventive thoughts.

The wellspring of inventive energy within me is eternal, continually refreshing with new and imaginative ideas.

I release any resistance to change, embracing inspiration that guides me to brilliance.

I am open to receiving inventive insights from unexpected sources and unlikely places.

The river of creative energy flows through me, carrying with it the seeds of new ideas.

Challenges serve as invitations to explore uncharted realms of inventive thinking.

Every idea I conceive is a stepping stone toward greater creativity and innovation.

My mind is a fertile ground for creative seeds to take root and flourish.

The canvas of my mind is painted with strokes of inventive brilliance, creating a vibrant masterpiece.

I welcome the chaos of creative exploration, knowing that within it lies the seeds of innovation.

My thoughts are seeds of potential, germinating into lush forests of inventive concepts.

I trust the serendipity of inventive discovery, finding beauty in the unexpected.

Every obstacle is a stepping stone toward unlocking fresh and inventive solutions.

I trust in the dynamic nature of my thoughts, adapting and evolving with creativity.

My mind is an expansive playground where ideas frolic and intertwine.

The landscapes of my imagination are ever-expanding, offering new vistas for exploration.

I trust in the divine flow of creative energy, allowing inspiration to guide my actions.

Every idea is a spark that ignites the flame of innovation within me.

I am a vessel for creative energy, allowing it to flow through me and manifest in beautiful ways.

I celebrate the diversity of my creative expressions, recognizing each as a unique masterpiece.

My mind is a fertile ground for creative seeds to take root and flourish.

I trust the intuitive whispers of inspiration that guide me towards inspired actions.

I celebrate the diversity of my creative expressions, recognizing each as a valuable contribution.

My mind is a workshop of endless possibilities, crafting ideas into tangible expressions.

Every creative endeavor is a collaboration between my thoughts and the universal flow of inspiration.

I embrace the serendipity of creative discovery, finding beauty in the unexpected.

I celebrate the spontaneous dance of inspiration, leading me to groundbreaking discoveries.

Every moment is an opportunity for a fresh and ingenious concept.

My thoughts are a symphony of originality, creating harmonies that resonate with the universe.

Challenges are gateways to inventive problem-solving and creative growth.

I welcome the diversity of thoughts, fostering a rich tapestry of imaginative expressions.

The canvas of my mind is painted with strokes of ingenious brilliance.

I trust the ebb and flow of my creative energy, allowing it to adapt and evolve effortlessly.

In the sanctuary of my mind, creative sparks illuminate the darkness, revealing endless possibilities.

The symphony of my thoughts plays a melody of innovation that reverberates through my actions.

I release any fear of judgment, allowing my creative expressions to flow authentically.

I am a vessel for the universal energy of inspiration, channeling it into my creative pursuits.

My thoughts are like seeds planted in the soil of my mind, growing into flourishing fields of creativity.

The architecture of my mind is built with the bricks of inventive ideas and imaginative designs.

I trust that the universe supports and amplifies my creative endeavors.

I am a conductor orchestrating the harmonious melodies of creative thoughts and ideas.

The currents of creative energy flow through me, connecting me to the infinite reservoir of inspiration.

The kaleidoscope of ideas in my mind forms a rich mosaic of creative possibilities.

The symphony of inspiration orchestrates beautiful melodies in every area of my life.

I welcome the unexpected twists and turns of my creative path, trusting they lead to new opportunities.

Challenges are mere gateways to innovative solutions, and I navigate through them with ease.

The fertile ground of my thoughts nurtures seeds of creativity that blossom into unique expressions.

Challenges are mere stepping stones, guiding me towards unexplored realms of inventive solutions.

Every idea is a journey, and I embark on these creative adventures with enthusiasm and curiosity.

The landscapes of my imagination are ever-expanding, offering new vistas for exploration.

The alchemy of my mind transforms ordinary thoughts into extraordinary and innovative concepts.

My creative intuition is a guiding star, leading me towards uncharted territories of inspiration.

My mind is an open channel, inviting winds of inspiration to carry in new and novel concepts.

I embrace the cyclical nature of inventiveness, honoring periods of rest and reflection.

Challenges are opportunities for inventive problem-solving and creative evolution.

The architecture of my thoughts is built with the bricks of inventive ideas and original designs.

My mind is an open gateway for inspiration, inviting inventive ideas to flow freely.

The seeds of innovation planted in my thoughts germinate into flourishing fields of creativity.

I celebrate the dance of ideas in my mind, a choreography of inventive concepts.

The river of inspiration flows gracefully through me, carving new pathways and shaping my destiny.

Challenges are mere stepping stones, guiding me towards innovative solutions and growth.

I trust the serendipity of inventive discovery, finding beauty in the unexpected.

Every obstacle is an opportunity for my inventive nature to showcase resilience and resourcefulness.

The symphony of creativity orchestrates beautiful melodies in every area of my life.

I release any fear of judgment, allowing my inventive expressions to radiate with authenticity.

I am a vessel for the universal flow of inventive energy, shaping my reality with flair.

My mind is a fertile ground where seeds of innovation sprout into groundbreaking concepts.

I embrace the dance of creativity, letting it guide me to new and unexplored territories.

Innovative solutions reveal themselves effortlessly, like stars illuminating the night sky.

Challenges are invitations for my inventive spirit to shine brightly and find ingenious answers.

Every thought carries the potential to birth a novel idea, contributing to the tapestry of innovation.

The symphony of my thoughts resonates with the harmonious chords of originality.

I am a conduit for inventive energy, channeling it into every aspect of my life.

The landscape of my mind is an ever-evolving canvas painted with strokes of ingenious ideas.

In the playground of my imagination, I joyfully explore the infinite realms of inventiveness.

I welcome the unpredictable nature of creative exploration, finding joy in the unexpected.

The canvas of my mind is painted with strokes of inventive brilliance, creating a vibrant masterpiece.

I welcome the chaos of creative exploration, knowing that within it lies the seeds of innovation.

My thoughts are seeds of potential, germinating into lush forests of inventive concepts.

I trust the serendipity of inventive discovery, finding beauty in the unexpected.

I am a magnet for inspiration, attracting inventive ideas effortlessly and naturally.

The symphony of creativity orchestrates beautiful melodies in every area of my life.

I release any fear of judgment, allowing my inventive expressions to radiate with authenticity.

I am a vessel for the universal flow of inventive energy, shaping my reality with flair.

My mind is a boundless canvas, ready to capture the brushstrokes of inspired thoughts.

The fountain of inventive ideas within me is boundless and ever-flowing.

I trust the serendipity of inventive discovery, finding beauty in the unexpected.

I am a magnet for inspiration, attracting inventive ideas effortlessly and naturally.

The symphony of creativity orchestrates beautiful melodies in every area of my life.

I release any fear of judgment, allowing my inventive expressions to radiate with authenticity.

I am a vessel for the universal flow of inventive energy, shaping my reality with flair.

Every creative endeavor is a tapestry woven with threads of innovation and ingenuity.

I celebrate the dance of ideas in my mind, a choreography of inventive thoughts.

The wellspring of inventive energy within me is eternal, continually refreshing with new and imaginative ideas.

I trust in the infinite intelligence of my inventive mind, guiding me towards unique expressions.

I am an artist of thoughts, sculpting ideas into tangible and impactful forms.

I release any self-imposed limitations, allowing my inventive thoughts to soar to new heights.

The river of inspiration flows through me, carving new pathways and shaping my destiny.

Every creative endeavor is a tapestry woven with threads of innovation and ingenuity.

I celebrate the dance of ideas in my mind, a choreography of inventive thoughts.

The wellspring of inventive energy within me is eternal, continually refreshing with new and imaginative ideas.

I trust in the infinite intelligence of my inventive mind, guiding me towards unique expressions.

I am an artist of thoughts, sculpting ideas into tangible and impactful forms.

The canvas of my mind is painted with strokes of inventive brilliance, creating a vibrant masterpiece.

I welcome the chaos of creative exploration, knowing that within it lies the seeds of innovation.

My thoughts are seeds of potential, germinating into lush forests of inventive concepts.

I release any self-imposed limitations, allowing my inventive thoughts to soar to new heights.

The river of inspiration flows through me, carving new pathways and shaping my destiny.

Every creative endeavor is a tapestry woven with threads of innovation and ingenuity.

I celebrate the dance of ideas in my mind, a choreography of inventive thoughts.

The wellspring of inventive energy within me is eternal, continually refreshing with new and imaginative ideas.

I trust in the infinite intelligence of my inventive mind, guiding me towards unique expressions.

I am an artist of thoughts, sculpting ideas into tangible and impactful forms.

The canvas of my mind is painted with strokes of inventive brilliance, creating a vibrant masterpiece.

I welcome the chaos of creative exploration, knowing that within it lies the seeds of innovation.

My thoughts are seeds of potential, germinating into lush forests of inventive concepts.

I am an artist of thoughts, sculpting ideas into tangible and impactful forms.

The canvas of my mind is painted with strokes of inventive brilliance, creating a vibrant masterpiece.

I welcome the chaos of creative exploration, knowing that within it lies the seeds of innovation.

My thoughts are seeds of potential, germinating into lush forests of inventive concepts.

I trust the serendipity of inventive discovery, finding beauty in the unexpected.

I am a magnet for inspiration, attracting inventive ideas effortlessly and naturally.

The symphony of creativity orchestrates beautiful melodies in every area of my life.

I release any fear of judgment, allowing my inventive expressions to radiate with authenticity.

I am a vessel for the universal flow of inventive energy, shaping my reality with flair.

My mind is a boundless canvas, ready to capture the brushstrokes of inspired thoughts.

The symphony of creativity orchestrates beautiful melodies in every area of my life.

I release any fear of judgment, allowing my inventive expressions to radiate with authenticity.

I am a vessel for the universal flow of inventive energy, shaping my reality with flair.

My mind is a boundless canvas, ready to capture the brushstrokes of inspired thoughts.

I release any self-imposed limitations, allowing my inventive thoughts to soar to new heights.

The river of inspiration flows through me, carving new pathways and shaping my destiny.

Every creative endeavor is a tapestry woven with threads of innovation and ingenuity.

I celebrate the dance of ideas in my mind, a choreography of inventive thoughts.

The wellspring of inventive energy within me is eternal, continually refreshing with new and imaginative ideas.

I trust in the infinite intelligence of my inventive mind, guiding me towards unique expressions.

My creative essence is a guiding force, fueling my journey towards new horizons.

I trust the serendipity of inventive discovery, finding beauty in the unexpected.

I am a magnet for inspiration, attracting inventive ideas effortlessly and naturally.

The symphony of creativity orchestrates beautiful melodies in every area of my life.

I release any fear of judgment, allowing my inventive expressions to radiate with authenticity.

I am a vessel for the universal flow of inventive energy, shaping my reality with flair.

My mind is a boundless canvas, ready to capture the brushstrokes of inspired thoughts.

I release any self-imposed limitations, allowing my inventive thoughts to soar to new heights.

I trust the serendipity of inventive discovery, finding beauty in the unexpected.

I am a magnet for inspiration, attracting inventive ideas effortlessly and naturally.

I am a conduit for the universal flow of creative energy, channeling inspiration into my endeavors.

The tapestry of my thoughts is woven with threads of imaginative brilliance and ingenuity.

I release any fear of judgment and allow my creative expressions to flow authentically.

I am a vessel for the magic of inventive inspiration, and it flows through me effortlessly.

Challenges are opportunities for my inventive nature to shine.

The playground of my thoughts is a breeding ground for originality and creativity.

I welcome the unfolding of my imaginative potential in every moment.

Challenges are stepping stones, guiding me toward ingenious breakthroughs.

The tapestry of my ideas weaves together a rich mosaic of inventive possibilities.

I trust in the spontaneous dance of my thoughts, leading to innovative insights.

I trust the process of creative evolution, embracing each stage with openness and curiosity.

I am a conduit for the universal flow of creative energy, channeling inspiration into my endeavors.

The tapestry of my thoughts is woven with threads of imaginative brilliance and ingenuity.

I release any fear of judgment and allow my creative expressions to flow authentically.

I am a vessel for the magic of inventive inspiration, and it flows through me effortlessly.

My creative spirit is resilient, overcoming challenges with inventive solutions.

Every moment is an opportunity for creative expression and artistic exploration.

I am an architect of inventive ideas, constructing a reality that reflects my imaginative vision.

My mind is a fertile ground where ideas germinate, grow, and blossom into innovative concepts.

I trust the process of creative evolution, embracing each stage with openness and curiosity.

I embrace the beauty of uncertainty, knowing it often leads to profound moments of inspiration.

My mind is a sanctuary for innovative thoughts, where ideas bloom and flourish.

I welcome the flow of inventive energy, allowing it to inspire and uplift me.

I am open to creative breakthroughs that lead to new and exciting possibilities.

Challenges are invitations to tap into the well of inventive inspiration within me.

Every idea I conceive is a spark that ignites the flame of innovation within my soul.

My creative essence is resilient, overcoming challenges with inventive solutions.

Every moment is an opportunity for creative expression and artistic exploration.

I am an architect of inventive ideas, constructing a reality that reflects my imaginative vision.

My mind is a fertile ground where ideas germinate, grow, and blossom into innovative concepts.

The symphony of my inventive mind resonates with the harmonious frequencies of creativity.

I release any resistance to change, embracing inspiration that guides me to brilliance.

I am open to receiving inventive insights from unexpected sources and unlikely places.

The river of creative energy flows through me, carrying with it the seeds of new ideas.

Challenges serve as invitations to explore uncharted realms of inventive thinking.

Every idea I conceive is a stepping stone toward greater creativity and innovation.

My mind is a fertile ground for creative seeds to take root and flourish.

I trust the intuitive whispers of inventive inspiration that guide me toward inspired actions.

Challenges are opportunities for creative exploration and ingenious problem-solving.

The canvas of my life is painted with strokes of inventive brilliance and originality.

My thoughts are seeds of potential, germinating into lush forests of inventive concepts.

My mind is a wellspring of creative ideas and innovative solutions.

I effortlessly tap into my creative reservoir to generate inventive concepts.

Every challenge is an opportunity for my inventive nature to shine.

The playground of my thoughts is a breeding ground for originality and creativity.

I welcome the unfolding of my imaginative potential in every moment.

Challenges are stepping stones, guiding me toward ingenious breakthroughs.

The tapestry of my ideas weaves together a rich mosaic of inventive possibilities.

I trust in the spontaneous dance of my thoughts, leading to innovative insights.

My creative essence is a guiding force, fueling my journey towards new horizons.

The symphony of creativity resonates within me, guiding me towards inventive and ingenious solutions.

I welcome the unknown with excitement, trusting that creativity will illuminate the path ahead.

Every challenge is an opportunity for innovative problem-solving and creative growth.

I celebrate the dance of ideas in my mind, a choreography of inventive thoughts.

The wellspring of inventive energy within me is eternal, continually refreshing with new and imaginative ideas.

I trust in the infinite intelligence of my inventive mind, guiding me towards unique expressions.

I am an artist of thoughts, sculpting ideas into tangible and impactful forms.

The canvas of my mind is painted with strokes of inventive brilliance, creating a vibrant masterpiece.

I welcome the chaos of creative exploration, knowing that within it lies the seeds of innovation.

My thoughts are seeds of potential, germinating into lush forests of inventive concepts.

I release any fear of judgment, allowing my inventive expressions to shine authentically.

I am a vessel for the universal flow of inventive energy, shaping my reality with flair.

My mind is an open channel, inviting winds of inspiration to carry in new and novel concepts.

I embrace the cyclical nature of creativity, honoring periods of rest and reflection.

Challenges are mere stepping stones to innovative solutions and creative evolution.

The architecture of my thoughts is built with the bricks of inventive ideas and original designs.

I celebrate the kaleidoscope of ideas, recognizing each as a valuable contribution to my creativity.

My mind is a workshop where thoughts are sculpted into tangible expressions of ingenuity.

Every creative endeavor is a collaboration between my thoughts and the universal flow of inspiration.

I trust in the synchronicity of my inventive thoughts, leading me towards inspired actions.

I am an artist of thoughts, sculpting ideas into tangible and impactful forms.

The canvas of my mind is painted with strokes of inventive brilliance, creating a vibrant masterpiece.

I welcome the chaos of creative exploration, knowing that within it lies the seeds of innovation.

The essence of my thoughts is transformative, shaping my surroundings with inventive energy.

In my mental workshop, ideas are crafted into tangible expressions of ingenuity.

The symphony of my thoughts plays melodies that reverberate with inventive inspiration.

I am a conductor of innovative ideas, orchestrating a harmonious flow in my mind.

I welcome the dynamic interplay of ideas, blending them into a mosaic of creativity.

Every idea is a brushstroke painting the canvas of my mind with vibrant and imaginative hues.

I trust that the universe supports and amplifies my creative thought processes.

The symphony of creativity orchestrates beautiful melodies in every area of my life.

I release any fear of judgment, allowing my inventive expressions to radiate with authenticity.

I am a vessel for the universal flow of inventive energy, shaping my reality with flair.

My mind is a boundless canvas, ready to capture the brushstrokes of inspired thoughts.

I release any self-imposed limitations, allowing my inventive thoughts to soar to new heights.

The river of inspiration flows through me, carving new pathways and shaping my destiny.

Every creative endeavor is a tapestry woven with threads of innovation and ingenuity.

I celebrate the dance of ideas in my mind, a choreography of inventive thoughts.

The wellspring of inventive energy within me is eternal, continually refreshing with new and imaginative ideas.

I trust in the infinite intelligence of my inventive mind, guiding me toward unique expressions.

The symphony of my thoughts creates a melody of inspiration that echoes in my actions.

Challenges are gateways to creative solutions, and I navigate them with inventive flair.

The landscapes of my imagination continually evolve, offering new realms for exploration.

I release any limitations, allowing my thoughts to soar into innovative heights.

I celebrate the spontaneous dance of ideas in my mind, a ballet of inventiveness.

The river of inspiration flows gracefully through me, carving pathways of creative expression.

Every challenge is an opportunity to showcase my inventive and resourceful nature.

I trust in the serendipity of creative discovery, finding beauty in the unexpected.

I trust the serendipity of inventive discovery, finding beauty in the unexpected.

I am a magnet for inspiration, attracting inventive ideas effortlessly and naturally.

I am a magnet for inspiration, attracting inventive ideas effortlessly and naturally.

The symphony of creativity orchestrates beautiful melodies in every area of my life.

I release any fear of judgment, allowing my inventive expressions to radiate with authenticity.

I am a vessel for the universal flow of inventive energy, shaping my reality with flair.

My mind is a boundless canvas, ready to capture the brushstrokes of inspired thoughts.

I release any self-imposed limitations, allowing my inventive thoughts to soar to new heights.

The river of inspiration flows through me, carving new pathways and shaping my destiny.

Every creative endeavor is a tapestry woven with threads of innovation and ingenuity.

I celebrate the dance of ideas in my mind, a choreography of inventive thoughts.

The wellspring of inventive energy within me is eternal, continually refreshing with new and imaginative ideas.

I release any resistance to change, embracing inspiration that guides me to brilliance.

I am open to receiving inventive insights from unexpected sources and unlikely places.

The river of creative energy flows through me, carrying with it the seeds of new ideas.

Challenges serve as invitations to explore uncharted realms of inventive thinking.

Every idea I conceive is a stepping stone toward greater creativity and innovation.

My mind is a fertile ground for creative seeds to take root and flourish.

The canvas of my mind is painted with strokes of inventive brilliance, creating a vibrant masterpiece.

I welcome the chaos of creative exploration, knowing that within it lies the seeds of innovation.

My thoughts are seeds of potential, germinating into lush forests of inventive concepts.

I trust the serendipity of inventive discovery, finding beauty in the unexpected.

Every obstacle is a stepping stone toward unlocking fresh and inventive solutions.

I trust in the dynamic nature of my thoughts, adapting and evolving with creativity.

My mind is an expansive playground where ideas frolic and intertwine.

The landscapes of my imagination are ever-expanding, offering new vistas for exploration.

I trust in the divine flow of creative energy, allowing inspiration to guide my actions.

Every idea is a spark that ignites the flame of innovation within me.

I am a vessel for creative energy, allowing it to flow through me and manifest in beautiful ways.

I celebrate the diversity of my creative expressions, recognizing each as a unique masterpiece.

My mind is a fertile ground for creative seeds to take root and flourish.

I trust the intuitive whispers of inspiration that guide me towards inspired actions.

I celebrate the diversity of my creative expressions, recognizing each as a valuable contribution.

My mind is a workshop of endless possibilities, crafting ideas into tangible expressions.

Every creative endeavor is a collaboration between my thoughts and the universal flow of inspiration.

I embrace the serendipity of creative discovery, finding beauty in the unexpected.

I celebrate the spontaneous dance of inspiration, leading me to groundbreaking discoveries.

Every moment is an opportunity for a fresh and ingenious concept.

My thoughts are a symphony of originality, creating harmonies that resonate with the universe.

Challenges are gateways to inventive problem-solving and creative growth.

I welcome the diversity of thoughts, fostering a rich tapestry of imaginative expressions.

The canvas of my mind is painted with strokes of ingenious brilliance.

I trust the ebb and flow of my creative energy, allowing it to adapt and evolve effortlessly.

In the sanctuary of my mind, creative sparks illuminate the darkness, revealing endless possibilities.

The symphony of my thoughts plays a melody of innovation that reverberates through my actions.

I release any fear of judgment, allowing my creative expressions to flow authentically.

I am a vessel for the universal energy of inspiration, channeling it into my creative pursuits.

My thoughts are like seeds planted in the soil of my mind, growing into flourishing fields of creativity.

The architecture of my mind is built with the bricks of inventive ideas and imaginative designs.

I trust that the universe supports and amplifies my creative endeavors.

I am a conductor orchestrating the harmonious melodies of creative thoughts and ideas.

The currents of creative energy flow through me, connecting me to the infinite reservoir of inspiration.

The kaleidoscope of ideas in my mind forms a rich mosaic of creative possibilities.

The symphony of inspiration orchestrates beautiful melodies in every area of my life.

I welcome the unexpected twists and turns of my creative path, trusting they lead to new opportunities.

Challenges are mere gateways to innovative solutions, and I navigate through them with ease.

The fertile ground of my thoughts nurtures seeds of creativity that blossom into unique expressions.

Challenges are mere stepping stones, guiding me towards unexplored realms of inventive solutions.

Every idea is a journey, and I embark on these creative adventures with enthusiasm and curiosity.

The landscapes of my imagination are ever-expanding, offering new vistas for exploration.

The alchemy of my mind transforms ordinary thoughts into extraordinary and innovative concepts.

My creative intuition is a guiding star, leading me towards uncharted territories of inspiration.

My mind is an open channel, inviting winds of inspiration to carry in new and novel concepts.

I embrace the cyclical nature of inventiveness, honoring periods of rest and reflection.

Challenges are opportunities for inventive problem-solving and creative evolution.

The architecture of my thoughts is built with the bricks of inventive ideas and original designs.

My mind is an open gateway for inspiration, inviting inventive ideas to flow freely.

The seeds of innovation planted in my thoughts germinate into flourishing fields of creativity.

I celebrate the dance of ideas in my mind, a choreography of inventive concepts.

The river of inspiration flows gracefully through me, carving new pathways and shaping my destiny.

Challenges are mere stepping stones, guiding me towards innovative solutions and growth.

I trust the serendipity of inventive discovery, finding beauty in the unexpected.

Every obstacle is an opportunity for my inventive nature to showcase resilience and resourcefulness.

The symphony of creativity orchestrates beautiful melodies in every area of my life.

I release any fear of judgment, allowing my inventive expressions to radiate with authenticity.

I am a vessel for the universal flow of inventive energy, shaping my reality with flair.

My mind is a fertile ground where seeds of innovation sprout into groundbreaking concepts.

I embrace the dance of creativity, letting it guide me to new and unexplored territories.

Innovative solutions reveal themselves effortlessly, like stars illuminating the night sky.

Challenges are invitations for my inventive spirit to shine brightly and find ingenious answers.

Every thought carries the potential to birth a novel idea, contributing to the tapestry of innovation.

The symphony of my thoughts resonates with the harmonious chords of originality.

I am a conduit for inventive energy, channeling it into every aspect of my life.

The landscape of my mind is an ever-evolving canvas painted with strokes of ingenious ideas.

In the playground of my imagination, I joyfully explore the infinite realms of inventiveness.

I welcome the unpredictable nature of creative exploration, finding joy in the unexpected.

The canvas of my mind is painted with strokes of inventive brilliance, creating a vibrant masterpiece.

I welcome the chaos of creative exploration, knowing that within it lies the seeds of innovation.

My thoughts are seeds of potential, germinating into lush forests of inventive concepts.

I trust the serendipity of inventive discovery, finding beauty in the unexpected.

I am a magnet for inspiration, attracting inventive ideas effortlessly and naturally.

The symphony of creativity orchestrates beautiful melodies in every area of my life.

I release any fear of judgment, allowing my inventive expressions to radiate with authenticity.

I am a vessel for the universal flow of inventive energy, shaping my reality with flair.

My mind is a boundless canvas, ready to capture the brushstrokes of inspired thoughts.

The fountain of inventive ideas within me is boundless and ever-flowing.

I trust the serendipity of inventive discovery, finding beauty in the unexpected.

I am a magnet for inspiration, attracting inventive ideas effortlessly and naturally.

The symphony of creativity orchestrates beautiful melodies in every area of my life.

I release any fear of judgment, allowing my inventive expressions to radiate with authenticity.

I am a vessel for the universal flow of inventive energy, shaping my reality with flair.

Every creative endeavor is a tapestry woven with threads of innovation and ingenuity.

I celebrate the dance of ideas in my mind, a choreography of inventive thoughts.

The wellspring of inventive energy within me is eternal, continually refreshing with new and imaginative ideas.

I trust in the infinite intelligence of my inventive mind, guiding me towards unique expressions.

I am an artist of thoughts, sculpting ideas into tangible and impactful forms.

I release any self-imposed limitations, allowing my inventive thoughts to soar to new heights.

The river of inspiration flows through me, carving new pathways and shaping my destiny.

Every creative endeavor is a tapestry woven with threads of innovation and ingenuity.

I celebrate the dance of ideas in my mind, a choreography of inventive thoughts.

The wellspring of inventive energy within me is eternal, continually refreshing with new and imaginative ideas.

I trust in the infinite intelligence of my inventive mind, guiding me towards unique expressions.

I am an artist of thoughts, sculpting ideas into tangible and impactful forms.

The canvas of my mind is painted with strokes of inventive brilliance, creating a vibrant masterpiece.

I welcome the chaos of creative exploration, knowing that within it lies the seeds of innovation.

My thoughts are seeds of potential, germinating into lush forests of inventive concepts.

I release any self-imposed limitations, allowing my inventive thoughts to soar to new heights.

The river of inspiration flows through me, carving new pathways and shaping my destiny.

Every creative endeavor is a tapestry woven with threads of innovation and ingenuity.

I celebrate the dance of ideas in my mind, a choreography of inventive thoughts.

The wellspring of inventive energy within me is eternal, continually refreshing with new and imaginative ideas.

I trust in the infinite intelligence of my inventive mind, guiding me towards unique expressions.

I am an artist of thoughts, sculpting ideas into tangible and impactful forms.

The canvas of my mind is painted with strokes of inventive brilliance, creating a vibrant masterpiece.

I welcome the chaos of creative exploration, knowing that within it lies the seeds of innovation.

My thoughts are seeds of potential, germinating into lush forests of inventive concepts.

I am an artist of thoughts, sculpting ideas into tangible and impactful forms.

The canvas of my mind is painted with strokes of inventive brilliance, creating a vibrant masterpiece.

I welcome the chaos of creative exploration, knowing that within it lies the seeds of innovation.

My thoughts are seeds of potential, germinating into lush forests of inventive concepts.

I trust the serendipity of inventive discovery, finding beauty in the unexpected.

I am a magnet for inspiration, attracting inventive ideas effortlessly and naturally.

The symphony of creativity orchestrates beautiful melodies in every area of my life.

I release any fear of judgment, allowing my inventive expressions to radiate with authenticity.

I am a vessel for the universal flow of inventive energy, shaping my reality with flair.

My mind is a boundless canvas, ready to capture the brushstrokes of inspired thoughts.

The symphony of creativity orchestrates beautiful melodies in every area of my life.

I release any fear of judgment, allowing my inventive expressions to radiate with authenticity.

I am a vessel for the universal flow of inventive energy, shaping my reality with flair.

My mind is a boundless canvas, ready to capture the brushstrokes of inspired thoughts.

I release any self-imposed limitations, allowing my inventive thoughts to soar to new heights.

The river of inspiration flows through me, carving new pathways and shaping my destiny.

Every creative endeavor is a tapestry woven with threads of innovation and ingenuity.

I celebrate the dance of ideas in my mind, a choreography of inventive thoughts.

The wellspring of inventive energy within me is eternal, continually refreshing with new and imaginative ideas.

I trust in the infinite intelligence of my inventive mind, guiding me towards unique expressions.

My creative essence is a guiding force, fueling my journey towards new horizons.

I trust the serendipity of inventive discovery, finding beauty in the unexpected.

I am a magnet for inspiration, attracting inventive ideas effortlessly and naturally.

The symphony of creativity orchestrates beautiful melodies in every area of my life.

I release any fear of judgment, allowing my inventive expressions to radiate with authenticity.

I am a vessel for the universal flow of inventive energy, shaping my reality with flair.

My mind is a boundless canvas, ready to capture the brushstrokes of inspired thoughts.

I release any self-imposed limitations, allowing my inventive thoughts to soar to new heights.

I trust the serendipity of inventive discovery, finding beauty in the unexpected.

I am a magnet for inspiration, attracting inventive ideas effortlessly and naturally.

I am a conduit for the universal flow of creative energy, channeling inspiration into my endeavors.

The tapestry of my thoughts is woven with threads of imaginative brilliance and ingenuity.

I release any fear of judgment and allow my creative expressions to flow authentically.

I am a vessel for the magic of inventive inspiration, and it flows through me effortlessly.

Challenges are opportunities for my inventive nature to shine.

The playground of my thoughts is a breeding ground for originality and creativity.

I welcome the unfolding of my imaginative potential in every moment.

Challenges are stepping stones, guiding me toward ingenious breakthroughs.

The tapestry of my ideas weaves together a rich mosaic of inventive possibilities.

I trust in the spontaneous dance of my thoughts, leading to innovative insights.

I trust the process of creative evolution, embracing each stage with openness and curiosity.

I am a conduit for the universal flow of creative energy, channeling inspiration into my endeavors.

The tapestry of my thoughts is woven with threads of imaginative brilliance and ingenuity.

I release any fear of judgment and allow my creative expressions to flow authentically.

I am a vessel for the magic of inventive inspiration, and it flows through me effortlessly.

My creative spirit is resilient, overcoming challenges with inventive solutions.

Every moment is an opportunity for creative expression and artistic exploration.

I am an architect of inventive ideas, constructing a reality that reflects my imaginative vision.

My mind is a fertile ground where ideas germinate, grow, and blossom into innovative concepts.

I trust the process of creative evolution, embracing each stage with openness and curiosity.

I embrace the beauty of uncertainty, knowing it often leads to profound moments of inspiration.

My mind is a sanctuary for innovative thoughts, where ideas bloom and flourish.

I welcome the flow of inventive energy, allowing it to inspire and uplift me.

I am open to creative breakthroughs that lead to new and exciting possibilities.

Challenges are invitations to tap into the well of inventive inspiration within me.

Every idea I conceive is a spark that ignites the flame of innovation within my soul.

My creative essence is resilient, overcoming challenges with inventive solutions.

Every moment is an opportunity for creative expression and artistic exploration.

I am an architect of inventive ideas, constructing a reality that reflects my imaginative vision.

My mind is a fertile ground where ideas germinate, grow, and blossom into innovative concepts.

The symphony of my inventive mind resonates with the harmonious frequencies of creativity.

I release any resistance to change, embracing inspiration that guides me to brilliance.

I am open to receiving inventive insights from unexpected sources and unlikely places.

The river of creative energy flows through me, carrying with it the seeds of new ideas.

Challenges serve as invitations to explore uncharted realms of inventive thinking.

Every idea I conceive is a stepping stone toward greater creativity and innovation.

My mind is a fertile ground for creative seeds to take root and flourish.

I trust the intuitive whispers of inventive inspiration that guide me toward inspired actions.

Challenges are opportunities for creative exploration and ingenious problem-solving.

The canvas of my life is painted with strokes of inventive brilliance and originality.

My thoughts are seeds of potential, germinating into lush forests of inventive concepts.

My mind is a wellspring of creative ideas and innovative solutions.

I effortlessly tap into my creative reservoir to generate inventive concepts.

Every challenge is an opportunity for my inventive nature to shine.

The playground of my thoughts is a breeding ground for originality and creativity.

I welcome the unfolding of my imaginative potential in every moment.

Challenges are stepping stones, guiding me toward ingenious breakthroughs.

The tapestry of my ideas weaves together a rich mosaic of inventive possibilities.

I trust in the spontaneous dance of my thoughts, leading to innovative insights.

My creative essence is a guiding force, fueling my journey towards new horizons.

The symphony of creativity resonates within me, guiding me towards inventive and ingenious solutions.

I welcome the unknown with excitement, trusting that creativity will illuminate the path ahead.

Every challenge is an opportunity for innovative problem-solving and creative growth.

I celebrate the dance of ideas in my mind, a choreography of inventive thoughts.

The wellspring of inventive energy within me is eternal, continually refreshing with new and imaginative ideas.

I trust in the infinite intelligence of my inventive mind, guiding me towards unique expressions.

I am an artist of thoughts, sculpting ideas into tangible and impactful forms.

The canvas of my mind is painted with strokes of inventive brilliance, creating a vibrant masterpiece.

I welcome the chaos of creative exploration, knowing that within it lies the seeds of innovation.

My thoughts are seeds of potential, germinating into lush forests of inventive concepts.

I release any fear of judgment, allowing my inventive expressions to shine authentically.

I am a vessel for the universal flow of inventive energy, shaping my reality with flair.

My mind is an open channel, inviting winds of inspiration to carry in new and novel concepts.

I embrace the cyclical nature of creativity, honoring periods of rest and reflection.

Challenges are mere stepping stones to innovative solutions and creative evolution.

The architecture of my thoughts is built with the bricks of inventive ideas and original designs.

I celebrate the kaleidoscope of ideas, recognizing each as a valuable contribution to my creativity.

My mind is a workshop where thoughts are sculpted into tangible expressions of ingenuity.

Every creative endeavor is a collaboration between my thoughts and the universal flow of inspiration.

I trust in the synchronicity of my inventive thoughts, leading me towards inspired actions.

I am an artist of thoughts, sculpting ideas into tangible and impactful forms.

The canvas of my mind is painted with strokes of inventive brilliance, creating a vibrant masterpiece.

I welcome the chaos of creative exploration, knowing that within it lies the seeds of innovation.

The essence of my thoughts is transformative, shaping my surroundings with inventive energy.

In my mental workshop, ideas are crafted into tangible expressions of ingenuity.

The symphony of my thoughts plays melodies that reverberate with inventive inspiration.

I am a conductor of innovative ideas, orchestrating a harmonious flow in my mind.

I welcome the dynamic interplay of ideas, blending them into a mosaic of creativity.

Every idea is a brushstroke painting the canvas of my mind with vibrant and imaginative hues.

I trust that the universe supports and amplifies my creative thought processes.

The symphony of creativity orchestrates beautiful melodies in every area of my life.

I release any fear of judgment, allowing my inventive expressions to radiate with authenticity.

I am a vessel for the universal flow of inventive energy, shaping my reality with flair.

My mind is a boundless canvas, ready to capture the brushstrokes of inspired thoughts.

I release any self-imposed limitations, allowing my inventive thoughts to soar to new heights.

The river of inspiration flows through me, carving new pathways and shaping my destiny.

Every creative endeavor is a tapestry woven with threads of innovation and ingenuity.

I celebrate the dance of ideas in my mind, a choreography of inventive thoughts.

The wellspring of inventive energy within me is eternal, continually refreshing with new and imaginative ideas.

I trust in the infinite intelligence of my inventive mind, guiding me toward unique expressions.

The symphony of my thoughts creates a melody of inspiration that echoes in my actions.

Challenges are gateways to creative solutions, and I navigate them with inventive flair.

The landscapes of my imagination continually evolve, offering new realms for exploration.

I release any limitations, allowing my thoughts to soar into innovative heights.

I celebrate the spontaneous dance of ideas in my mind, a ballet of inventiveness.

The river of inspiration flows gracefully through me, carving pathways of creative expression.

Every challenge is an opportunity to showcase my inventive and resourceful nature.

I trust in the serendipity of creative discovery, finding beauty in the unexpected.

I trust the serendipity of inventive discovery, finding beauty in the unexpected.

I am a magnet for inspiration, attracting inventive ideas effortlessly and naturally.

I am a magnet for inspiration, attracting inventive ideas effortlessly and naturally.

The symphony of creativity orchestrates beautiful melodies in every area of my life.

I release any fear of judgment, allowing my inventive expressions to radiate with authenticity.

I am a vessel for the universal flow of inventive energy, shaping my reality with flair.

My mind is a boundless canvas, ready to capture the brushstrokes of inspired thoughts.

I release any self-imposed limitations, allowing my inventive thoughts to soar to new heights.

The river of inspiration flows through me, carving new pathways and shaping my destiny.

Every creative endeavor is a tapestry woven with threads of innovation and ingenuity.

I celebrate the dance of ideas in my mind, a choreography of inventive thoughts.

The wellspring of inventive energy within me is eternal, continually refreshing with new and imaginative ideas.

I release any resistance to change, embracing inspiration that guides me to brilliance.

I am open to receiving inventive insights from unexpected sources and unlikely places.

The river of creative energy flows through me, carrying with it the seeds of new ideas.

Challenges serve as invitations to explore uncharted realms of inventive thinking.

Every idea I conceive is a stepping stone toward greater creativity and innovation.

My mind is a fertile ground for creative seeds to take root and flourish.

The canvas of my mind is painted with strokes of inventive brilliance, creating a vibrant masterpiece.

I welcome the chaos of creative exploration, knowing that within it lies the seeds of innovation.

My thoughts are seeds of potential, germinating into lush forests of inventive concepts.

I trust the serendipity of inventive discovery, finding beauty in the unexpected.

Every obstacle is a stepping stone toward unlocking fresh and inventive solutions.

I trust in the dynamic nature of my thoughts, adapting and evolving with creativity.

My mind is an expansive playground where ideas frolic and intertwine.

The landscapes of my imagination are ever-expanding, offering new vistas for exploration.

I trust in the divine flow of creative energy, allowing inspiration to guide my actions.

Every idea is a spark that ignites the flame of innovation within me.

I am a vessel for creative energy, allowing it to flow through me and manifest in beautiful ways.

I celebrate the diversity of my creative expressions, recognizing each as a unique masterpiece.

My mind is a fertile ground for creative seeds to take root and flourish.

I trust the intuitive whispers of inspiration that guide me towards inspired actions.

I celebrate the diversity of my creative expressions, recognizing each as a valuable contribution.

My mind is a workshop of endless possibilities, crafting ideas into tangible expressions.

Every creative endeavor is a collaboration between my thoughts and the universal flow of inspiration.

I embrace the serendipity of creative discovery, finding beauty in the unexpected.

I celebrate the spontaneous dance of inspiration, leading me to groundbreaking discoveries.

Every moment is an opportunity for a fresh and ingenious concept.

My thoughts are a symphony of originality, creating harmonies that resonate with the universe.

Challenges are gateways to inventive problem-solving and creative growth.

I welcome the diversity of thoughts, fostering a rich tapestry of imaginative expressions.

The canvas of my mind is painted with strokes of ingenious brilliance.

I trust the ebb and flow of my creative energy, allowing it to adapt and evolve effortlessly.

In the sanctuary of my mind, creative sparks illuminate the darkness, revealing endless possibilities.

The symphony of my thoughts plays a melody of innovation that reverberates through my actions.

I release any fear of judgment, allowing my creative expressions to flow authentically.

I am a vessel for the universal energy of inspiration, channeling it into my creative pursuits.

My thoughts are like seeds planted in the soil of my mind, growing into flourishing fields of creativity.

The architecture of my mind is built with the bricks of inventive ideas and imaginative designs.

I trust that the universe supports and amplifies my creative endeavors.

I am a conductor orchestrating the harmonious melodies of creative thoughts and ideas.

The currents of creative energy flow through me, connecting me to the infinite reservoir of inspiration.

The kaleidoscope of ideas in my mind forms a rich mosaic of creative possibilities.

The symphony of inspiration orchestrates beautiful melodies in every area of my life.

I welcome the unexpected twists and turns of my creative path, trusting they lead to new opportunities.

Challenges are mere gateways to innovative solutions, and I navigate through them with ease.

The fertile ground of my thoughts nurtures seeds of creativity that blossom into unique expressions.

Challenges are mere stepping stones, guiding me towards unexplored realms of inventive solutions.

Every idea is a journey, and I embark on these creative adventures with enthusiasm and curiosity.

The landscapes of my imagination are ever-expanding, offering new vistas for exploration.

The alchemy of my mind transforms ordinary thoughts into extraordinary and innovative concepts.

My creative intuition is a guiding star, leading me towards uncharted territories of inspiration.

My mind is an open channel, inviting winds of inspiration to carry in new and novel concepts.

I embrace the cyclical nature of inventiveness, honoring periods of rest and reflection.

Challenges are opportunities for inventive problem-solving and creative evolution.

The architecture of my thoughts is built with the bricks of inventive ideas and original designs.

My mind is an open gateway for inspiration, inviting inventive ideas to flow freely.

The seeds of innovation planted in my thoughts germinate into flourishing fields of creativity.

I celebrate the dance of ideas in my mind, a choreography of inventive concepts.

The river of inspiration flows gracefully through me, carving new pathways and shaping my destiny.

Challenges are mere stepping stones, guiding me towards innovative solutions and growth.

I trust the serendipity of inventive discovery, finding beauty in the unexpected.

Every obstacle is an opportunity for my inventive nature to showcase resilience and resourcefulness.

The symphony of creativity orchestrates beautiful melodies in every area of my life.

I release any fear of judgment, allowing my inventive expressions to radiate with authenticity.

I am a vessel for the universal flow of inventive energy, shaping my reality with flair.

My mind is a fertile ground where seeds of innovation sprout into groundbreaking concepts.

I embrace the dance of creativity, letting it guide me to new and unexplored territories.

Innovative solutions reveal themselves effortlessly, like stars illuminating the night sky.

Challenges are invitations for my inventive spirit to shine brightly and find ingenious answers.

Every thought carries the potential to birth a novel idea, contributing to the tapestry of innovation.

The symphony of my thoughts resonates with the harmonious chords of originality.

I am a conduit for inventive energy, channeling it into every aspect of my life.

The landscape of my mind is an ever-evolving canvas painted with strokes of ingenious ideas.

In the playground of my imagination, I joyfully explore the infinite realms of inventiveness.

I welcome the unpredictable nature of creative exploration, finding joy in the unexpected.

The canvas of my mind is painted with strokes of inventive brilliance, creating a vibrant masterpiece.

I welcome the chaos of creative exploration, knowing that within it lies the seeds of innovation.

My thoughts are seeds of potential, germinating into lush forests of inventive concepts.

I trust the serendipity of inventive discovery, finding beauty in the unexpected.

I am a magnet for inspiration, attracting inventive ideas effortlessly and naturally.

The symphony of creativity orchestrates beautiful melodies in every area of my life.

I release any fear of judgment, allowing my inventive expressions to radiate with authenticity.

I am a vessel for the universal flow of inventive energy, shaping my reality with flair.

My mind is a boundless canvas, ready to capture the brushstrokes of inspired thoughts.

The fountain of inventive ideas within me is boundless and ever-flowing.

I trust the serendipity of inventive discovery, finding beauty in the unexpected.

I am a magnet for inspiration, attracting inventive ideas effortlessly and naturally.

The symphony of creativity orchestrates beautiful melodies in every area of my life.

I release any fear of judgment, allowing my inventive expressions to radiate with authenticity.

I am a vessel for the universal flow of inventive energy, shaping my reality with flair.

Every creative endeavor is a tapestry woven with threads of innovation and ingenuity.

I celebrate the dance of ideas in my mind, a choreography of inventive thoughts.

The wellspring of inventive energy within me is eternal, continually refreshing with new and imaginative ideas.

I trust in the infinite intelligence of my inventive mind, guiding me towards unique expressions.

I am an artist of thoughts, sculpting ideas into tangible and impactful forms.

I release any self-imposed limitations, allowing my inventive thoughts to soar to new heights.

The river of inspiration flows through me, carving new pathways and shaping my destiny.

Every creative endeavor is a tapestry woven with threads of innovation and ingenuity.

I celebrate the dance of ideas in my mind, a choreography of inventive thoughts.

The wellspring of inventive energy within me is eternal, continually refreshing with new and imaginative ideas.

I trust in the infinite intelligence of my inventive mind, guiding me towards unique expressions.

I am an artist of thoughts, sculpting ideas into tangible and impactful forms.

The canvas of my mind is painted with strokes of inventive brilliance, creating a vibrant masterpiece.

I welcome the chaos of creative exploration, knowing that within it lies the seeds of innovation.

My thoughts are seeds of potential, germinating into lush forests of inventive concepts.

I release any self-imposed limitations, allowing my inventive thoughts to soar to new heights.

The river of inspiration flows through me, carving new pathways and shaping my destiny.

Every creative endeavor is a tapestry woven with threads of innovation and ingenuity.

I celebrate the dance of ideas in my mind, a choreography of inventive thoughts.

The wellspring of inventive energy within me is eternal, continually refreshing with new and imaginative ideas.

I trust in the infinite intelligence of my inventive mind, guiding me towards unique expressions.

I am an artist of thoughts, sculpting ideas into tangible and impactful forms.

The canvas of my mind is painted with strokes of inventive brilliance, creating a vibrant masterpiece.

I welcome the chaos of creative exploration, knowing that within it lies the seeds of innovation.

My thoughts are seeds of potential, germinating into lush forests of inventive concepts.

I am an artist of thoughts, sculpting ideas into tangible and impactful forms.

The canvas of my mind is painted with strokes of inventive brilliance, creating a vibrant masterpiece.

I welcome the chaos of creative exploration, knowing that within it lies the seeds of innovation.

My thoughts are seeds of potential, germinating into lush forests of inventive concepts.

I trust the serendipity of inventive discovery, finding beauty in the unexpected.

I am a magnet for inspiration, attracting inventive ideas effortlessly and naturally.

The symphony of creativity orchestrates beautiful melodies in every area of my life.

I release any fear of judgment, allowing my inventive expressions to radiate with authenticity.

I am a vessel for the universal flow of inventive energy, shaping my reality with flair.

My mind is a boundless canvas, ready to capture the brushstrokes of inspired thoughts.

The symphony of creativity orchestrates beautiful melodies in every area of my life.

I release any fear of judgment, allowing my inventive expressions to radiate with authenticity.

I am a vessel for the universal flow of inventive energy, shaping my reality with flair.

My mind is a boundless canvas, ready to capture the brushstrokes of inspired thoughts.

I release any self-imposed limitations, allowing my inventive thoughts to soar to new heights.

The river of inspiration flows through me, carving new pathways and shaping my destiny.

Every creative endeavor is a tapestry woven with threads of innovation and ingenuity.

I celebrate the dance of ideas in my mind, a choreography of inventive thoughts.

The wellspring of inventive energy within me is eternal, continually refreshing with new and imaginative ideas.

I trust in the infinite intelligence of my inventive mind, guiding me towards unique expressions.

My creative essence is a guiding force, fueling my journey towards new horizons.

I trust the serendipity of inventive discovery, finding beauty in the unexpected.

I am a magnet for inspiration, attracting inventive ideas effortlessly and naturally.

The symphony of creativity orchestrates beautiful melodies in every area of my life.

I release any fear of judgment, allowing my inventive expressions to radiate with authenticity.

I am a vessel for the universal flow of inventive energy, shaping my reality with flair.

My mind is a boundless canvas, ready to capture the brushstrokes of inspired thoughts.

I release any self-imposed limitations, allowing my inventive thoughts to soar to new heights.

I trust the serendipity of inventive discovery, finding beauty in the unexpected.

I am a magnet for inspiration, attracting inventive ideas effortlessly and naturally.

I am a conduit for the universal flow of creative energy, channeling inspiration into my endeavors.

The tapestry of my thoughts is woven with threads of imaginative brilliance and ingenuity.

I release any fear of judgment and allow my creative expressions to flow authentically.

I am a vessel for the magic of inventive inspiration, and it flows through me effortlessly.

Challenges are opportunities for my inventive nature to shine.

The playground of my thoughts is a breeding ground for originality and creativity.

I welcome the unfolding of my imaginative potential in every moment.

Challenges are stepping stones, guiding me toward ingenious breakthroughs.

The tapestry of my ideas weaves together a rich mosaic of inventive possibilities.

I trust in the spontaneous dance of my thoughts, leading to innovative insights.

I trust the process of creative evolution, embracing each stage with openness and curiosity.

I am a conduit for the universal flow of creative energy, channeling inspiration into my endeavors.

The tapestry of my thoughts is woven with threads of imaginative brilliance and ingenuity.

I release any fear of judgment and allow my creative expressions to flow authentically.

I am a vessel for the magic of inventive inspiration, and it flows through me effortlessly.

My creative spirit is resilient, overcoming challenges with inventive solutions.

Every moment is an opportunity for creative expression and artistic exploration.

I am an architect of inventive ideas, constructing a reality that reflects my imaginative vision.

My mind is a fertile ground where ideas germinate, grow, and blossom into innovative concepts.

I trust the process of creative evolution, embracing each stage with openness and curiosity.

I embrace the beauty of uncertainty, knowing it often leads to profound moments of inspiration.

My mind is a sanctuary for innovative thoughts, where ideas bloom and flourish.

I welcome the flow of inventive energy, allowing it to inspire and uplift me.

I am open to creative breakthroughs that lead to new and exciting possibilities.

Challenges are invitations to tap into the well of inventive inspiration within me.

Every idea I conceive is a spark that ignites the flame of innovation within my soul.

My creative essence is resilient, overcoming challenges with inventive solutions.

Every moment is an opportunity for creative expression and artistic exploration.

I am an architect of inventive ideas, constructing a reality that reflects my imaginative vision.

My mind is a fertile ground where ideas germinate, grow, and blossom into innovative concepts.

The symphony of my inventive mind resonates with the harmonious frequencies of creativity.

I release any resistance to change, embracing inspiration that guides me to brilliance.

I am open to receiving inventive insights from unexpected sources and unlikely places.

The river of creative energy flows through me, carrying with it the seeds of new ideas.

Challenges serve as invitations to explore uncharted realms of inventive thinking.

Every idea I conceive is a stepping stone toward greater creativity and innovation.

My mind is a fertile ground for creative seeds to take root and flourish.

I trust the intuitive whispers of inventive inspiration that guide me toward inspired actions.

Challenges are opportunities for creative exploration and ingenious problem-solving.

The canvas of my life is painted with strokes of inventive brilliance and originality.

My thoughts are seeds of potential, germinating into lush forests of inventive concepts.

My mind is a wellspring of creative ideas and innovative solutions.

I effortlessly tap into my creative reservoir to generate inventive concepts.

Every challenge is an opportunity for my inventive nature to shine.

The playground of my thoughts is a breeding ground for originality and creativity.

I welcome the unfolding of my imaginative potential in every moment.

Challenges are stepping stones, guiding me toward ingenious breakthroughs.

The tapestry of my ideas weaves together a rich mosaic of inventive possibilities.

I trust in the spontaneous dance of my thoughts, leading to innovative insights.

My creative essence is a guiding force, fueling my journey towards new horizons.

The symphony of creativity resonates within me, guiding me towards inventive and ingenious solutions.

I welcome the unknown with excitement, trusting that creativity will illuminate the path ahead.

Every challenge is an opportunity for innovative problem-solving and creative growth.

I celebrate the dance of ideas in my mind, a choreography of inventive thoughts.

The wellspring of inventive energy within me is eternal, continually refreshing with new and imaginative ideas.

I trust in the infinite intelligence of my inventive mind, guiding me towards unique expressions.

I am an artist of thoughts, sculpting ideas into tangible and impactful forms.

The canvas of my mind is painted with strokes of inventive brilliance, creating a vibrant masterpiece.

I welcome the chaos of creative exploration, knowing that within it lies the seeds of innovation.

My thoughts are seeds of potential, germinating into lush forests of inventive concepts.

I release any fear of judgment, allowing my inventive expressions to shine authentically.

I am a vessel for the universal flow of inventive energy, shaping my reality with flair.

My mind is an open channel, inviting winds of inspiration to carry in new and novel concepts.

I embrace the cyclical nature of creativity, honoring periods of rest and reflection.

Challenges are mere stepping stones to innovative solutions and creative evolution.

The architecture of my thoughts is built with the bricks of inventive ideas and original designs.

I celebrate the kaleidoscope of ideas, recognizing each as a valuable contribution to my creativity.

My mind is a workshop where thoughts are sculpted into tangible expressions of ingenuity.

Every creative endeavor is a collaboration between my thoughts and the universal flow of inspiration.

I trust in the synchronicity of my inventive thoughts, leading me towards inspired actions.

I am an artist of thoughts, sculpting ideas into tangible and impactful forms.

The canvas of my mind is painted with strokes of inventive brilliance, creating a vibrant masterpiece.

I welcome the chaos of creative exploration, knowing that within it lies the seeds of innovation.

The essence of my thoughts is transformative, shaping my surroundings with inventive energy.

In my mental workshop, ideas are crafted into tangible expressions of ingenuity.

The symphony of my thoughts plays melodies that reverberate with inventive inspiration.

I am a conductor of innovative ideas, orchestrating a harmonious flow in my mind.

I welcome the dynamic interplay of ideas, blending them into a mosaic of creativity.

Every idea is a brushstroke painting the canvas of my mind with vibrant and imaginative hues.

I trust that the universe supports and amplifies my creative thought processes.

The symphony of creativity orchestrates beautiful melodies in every area of my life.

I release any fear of judgment, allowing my inventive expressions to radiate with authenticity.

I am a vessel for the universal flow of inventive energy, shaping my reality with flair.

My mind is a boundless canvas, ready to capture the brushstrokes of inspired thoughts.

I release any self-imposed limitations, allowing my inventive thoughts to soar to new heights.

The river of inspiration flows through me, carving new pathways and shaping my destiny.

Every creative endeavor is a tapestry woven with threads of innovation and ingenuity.

I celebrate the dance of ideas in my mind, a choreography of inventive thoughts.

The wellspring of inventive energy within me is eternal, continually refreshing with new and imaginative ideas.

I trust in the infinite intelligence of my inventive mind, guiding me toward unique expressions.

The symphony of my thoughts creates a melody of inspiration that echoes in my actions.

Challenges are gateways to creative solutions, and I navigate them with inventive flair.

The landscapes of my imagination continually evolve, offering new realms for exploration.

I release any limitations, allowing my thoughts to soar into innovative heights.

I celebrate the spontaneous dance of ideas in my mind, a ballet of inventiveness.

The river of inspiration flows gracefully through me, carving pathways of creative expression.

Every challenge is an opportunity to showcase my inventive and resourceful nature.

I trust in the serendipity of creative discovery, finding beauty in the unexpected.

I trust the serendipity of inventive discovery, finding beauty in the unexpected.

I am a magnet for inspiration, attracting inventive ideas effortlessly and naturally.

I am a magnet for inspiration, attracting inventive ideas effortlessly and naturally.

The symphony of creativity orchestrates beautiful melodies in every area of my life.

I release any fear of judgment, allowing my inventive expressions to radiate with authenticity.

I am a vessel for the universal flow of inventive energy, shaping my reality with flair.

My mind is a boundless canvas, ready to capture the brushstrokes of inspired thoughts.

I release any self-imposed limitations, allowing my inventive thoughts to soar to new heights.

The river of inspiration flows through me, carving new pathways and shaping my destiny.

Every creative endeavor is a tapestry woven with threads of innovation and ingenuity.

I celebrate the dance of ideas in my mind, a choreography of inventive thoughts.

The wellspring of inventive energy within me is eternal, continually refreshing with new and imaginative ideas.

I release any resistance to change, embracing inspiration that guides me to brilliance.

I am open to receiving inventive insights from unexpected sources and unlikely places.

The river of creative energy flows through me, carrying with it the seeds of new ideas.

Challenges serve as invitations to explore uncharted realms of inventive thinking.

Every idea I conceive is a stepping stone toward greater creativity and innovation.

My mind is a fertile ground for creative seeds to take root and flourish.

The canvas of my mind is painted with strokes of inventive brilliance, creating a vibrant masterpiece.

I welcome the chaos of creative exploration, knowing that within it lies the seeds of innovation.

My thoughts are seeds of potential, germinating into lush forests of inventive concepts.

I trust the serendipity of inventive discovery, finding beauty in the unexpected.

Every obstacle is a stepping stone toward unlocking fresh and inventive solutions.

I trust in the dynamic nature of my thoughts, adapting and evolving with creativity.

My mind is an expansive playground where ideas frolic and intertwine.

The landscapes of my imagination are ever-expanding, offering new vistas for exploration.

I trust in the divine flow of creative energy, allowing inspiration to guide my actions.

Every idea is a spark that ignites the flame of innovation within me.

I am a vessel for creative energy, allowing it to flow through me and manifest in beautiful ways.

I celebrate the diversity of my creative expressions, recognizing each as a unique masterpiece.

My mind is a fertile ground for creative seeds to take root and flourish.

I trust the intuitive whispers of inspiration that guide me towards inspired actions.

I celebrate the diversity of my creative expressions, recognizing each as a valuable contribution.

My mind is a workshop of endless possibilities, crafting ideas into tangible expressions.

Every creative endeavor is a collaboration between my thoughts and the universal flow of inspiration.

I embrace the serendipity of creative discovery, finding beauty in the unexpected.

I celebrate the spontaneous dance of inspiration, leading me to groundbreaking discoveries.

Every moment is an opportunity for a fresh and ingenious concept.

My thoughts are a symphony of originality, creating harmonies that resonate with the universe.

Challenges are gateways to inventive problem-solving and creative growth.

I welcome the diversity of thoughts, fostering a rich tapestry of imaginative expressions.

The canvas of my mind is painted with strokes of ingenious brilliance.

I trust the ebb and flow of my creative energy, allowing it to adapt and evolve effortlessly.

In the sanctuary of my mind, creative sparks illuminate the darkness, revealing endless possibilities.

The symphony of my thoughts plays a melody of innovation that reverberates through my actions.

I release any fear of judgment, allowing my creative expressions to flow authentically.

I am a vessel for the universal energy of inspiration, channeling it into my creative pursuits.

My thoughts are like seeds planted in the soil of my mind, growing into flourishing fields of creativity.

The architecture of my mind is built with the bricks of inventive ideas and imaginative designs.

I trust that the universe supports and amplifies my creative endeavors.

I am a conductor orchestrating the harmonious melodies of creative thoughts and ideas.

The currents of creative energy flow through me, connecting me to the infinite reservoir of inspiration.

The kaleidoscope of ideas in my mind forms a rich mosaic of creative possibilities.

The symphony of inspiration orchestrates beautiful melodies in every area of my life.

I welcome the unexpected twists and turns of my creative path, trusting they lead to new opportunities.

Challenges are mere gateways to innovative solutions, and I navigate through them with ease.

The fertile ground of my thoughts nurtures seeds of creativity that blossom into unique expressions.

Challenges are mere stepping stones, guiding me towards unexplored realms of inventive solutions.

Every idea is a journey, and I embark on these creative adventures with enthusiasm and curiosity.

The landscapes of my imagination are ever-expanding, offering new vistas for exploration.

The alchemy of my mind transforms ordinary thoughts into extraordinary and innovative concepts.

My creative intuition is a guiding star, leading me towards uncharted territories of inspiration.

My mind is an open channel, inviting winds of inspiration to carry in new and novel concepts.

I embrace the cyclical nature of inventiveness, honoring periods of rest and reflection.

Challenges are opportunities for inventive problem-solving and creative evolution.

The architecture of my thoughts is built with the bricks of inventive ideas and original designs.

My mind is an open gateway for inspiration, inviting inventive ideas to flow freely.

The seeds of innovation planted in my thoughts germinate into flourishing fields of creativity.

I celebrate the dance of ideas in my mind, a choreography of inventive concepts.

The river of inspiration flows gracefully through me, carving new pathways and shaping my destiny.

Challenges are mere stepping stones, guiding me towards innovative solutions and growth.

I trust the serendipity of inventive discovery, finding beauty in the unexpected.

Every obstacle is an opportunity for my inventive nature to showcase resilience and resourcefulness.

The symphony of creativity orchestrates beautiful melodies in every area of my life.

I release any fear of judgment, allowing my inventive expressions to radiate with authenticity.

I am a vessel for the universal flow of inventive energy, shaping my reality with flair.

My mind is a fertile ground where seeds of innovation sprout into groundbreaking concepts.

I embrace the dance of creativity, letting it guide me to new and unexplored territories.

Innovative solutions reveal themselves effortlessly, like stars illuminating the night sky.

Challenges are invitations for my inventive spirit to shine brightly and find ingenious answers.

Every thought carries the potential to birth a novel idea, contributing to the tapestry of innovation.

The symphony of my thoughts resonates with the harmonious chords of originality.

I am a conduit for inventive energy, channeling it into every aspect of my life.

The landscape of my mind is an ever-evolving canvas painted with strokes of ingenious ideas.

In the playground of my imagination, I joyfully explore the infinite realms of inventiveness.

I welcome the unpredictable nature of creative exploration, finding joy in the unexpected.

The canvas of my mind is painted with strokes of inventive brilliance, creating a vibrant masterpiece.

I welcome the chaos of creative exploration, knowing that within it lies the seeds of innovation.

My thoughts are seeds of potential, germinating into lush forests of inventive concepts.

I trust the serendipity of inventive discovery, finding beauty in the unexpected.

I am a magnet for inspiration, attracting inventive ideas effortlessly and naturally.

The symphony of creativity orchestrates beautiful melodies in every area of my life.

I release any fear of judgment, allowing my inventive expressions to radiate with authenticity.

I am a vessel for the universal flow of inventive energy, shaping my reality with flair.

My mind is a boundless canvas, ready to capture the brushstrokes of inspired thoughts.

The fountain of inventive ideas within me is boundless and ever-flowing.

I trust the serendipity of inventive discovery, finding beauty in the unexpected.

I am a magnet for inspiration, attracting inventive ideas effortlessly and naturally.

The symphony of creativity orchestrates beautiful melodies in every area of my life.

I release any fear of judgment, allowing my inventive expressions to radiate with authenticity.

I am a vessel for the universal flow of inventive energy, shaping my reality with flair.

Every creative endeavor is a tapestry woven with threads of innovation and ingenuity.

I celebrate the dance of ideas in my mind, a choreography of inventive thoughts.

The wellspring of inventive energy within me is eternal, continually refreshing with new and imaginative ideas.

I trust in the infinite intelligence of my inventive mind, guiding me towards unique expressions.

I am an artist of thoughts, sculpting ideas into tangible and impactful forms.

I release any self-imposed limitations, allowing my inventive thoughts to soar to new heights.

The river of inspiration flows through me, carving new pathways and shaping my destiny.

Every creative endeavor is a tapestry woven with threads of innovation and ingenuity.

I celebrate the dance of ideas in my mind, a choreography of inventive thoughts.

The wellspring of inventive energy within me is eternal, continually refreshing with new and imaginative ideas.

I trust in the infinite intelligence of my inventive mind, guiding me towards unique expressions.

I am an artist of thoughts, sculpting ideas into tangible and impactful forms.

The canvas of my mind is painted with strokes of inventive brilliance, creating a vibrant masterpiece.

I welcome the chaos of creative exploration, knowing that within it lies the seeds of innovation.

My thoughts are seeds of potential, germinating into lush forests of inventive concepts.

I release any self-imposed limitations, allowing my inventive thoughts to soar to new heights.

The river of inspiration flows through me, carving new pathways and shaping my destiny.

Every creative endeavor is a tapestry woven with threads of innovation and ingenuity.

I celebrate the dance of ideas in my mind, a choreography of inventive thoughts.

The wellspring of inventive energy within me is eternal, continually refreshing with new and imaginative ideas.

I trust in the infinite intelligence of my inventive mind, guiding me towards unique expressions.

I am an artist of thoughts, sculpting ideas into tangible and impactful forms.

The canvas of my mind is painted with strokes of inventive brilliance, creating a vibrant masterpiece.

I welcome the chaos of creative exploration, knowing that within it lies the seeds of innovation.

My thoughts are seeds of potential, germinating into lush forests of inventive concepts.

I am an artist of thoughts, sculpting ideas into tangible and impactful forms.

The canvas of my mind is painted with strokes of inventive brilliance, creating a vibrant masterpiece.

I welcome the chaos of creative exploration, knowing that within it lies the seeds of innovation.

My thoughts are seeds of potential, germinating into lush forests of inventive concepts.

I trust the serendipity of inventive discovery, finding beauty in the unexpected.

I am a magnet for inspiration, attracting inventive ideas effortlessly and naturally.

The symphony of creativity orchestrates beautiful melodies in every area of my life.

I release any fear of judgment, allowing my inventive expressions to radiate with authenticity.

I am a vessel for the universal flow of inventive energy, shaping my reality with flair.

My mind is a boundless canvas, ready to capture the brushstrokes of inspired thoughts.

The symphony of creativity orchestrates beautiful melodies in every area of my life.

I release any fear of judgment, allowing my inventive expressions to radiate with authenticity.

I am a vessel for the universal flow of inventive energy, shaping my reality with flair.

My mind is a boundless canvas, ready to capture the brushstrokes of inspired thoughts.

I release any self-imposed limitations, allowing my inventive thoughts to soar to new heights.

The river of inspiration flows through me, carving new pathways and shaping my destiny.

Every creative endeavor is a tapestry woven with threads of innovation and ingenuity.

I celebrate the dance of ideas in my mind, a choreography of inventive thoughts.

The wellspring of inventive energy within me is eternal, continually refreshing with new and imaginative ideas.

I trust in the infinite intelligence of my inventive mind, guiding me towards unique expressions.

My creative essence is a guiding force, fueling my journey towards new horizons.

I trust the serendipity of inventive discovery, finding beauty in the unexpected.

I am a magnet for inspiration, attracting inventive ideas effortlessly and naturally.

The symphony of creativity orchestrates beautiful melodies in every area of my life.

I release any fear of judgment, allowing my inventive expressions to radiate with authenticity.

I am a vessel for the universal flow of inventive energy, shaping my reality with flair.

My mind is a boundless canvas, ready to capture the brushstrokes of inspired thoughts.

I release any self-imposed limitations, allowing my inventive thoughts to soar to new heights.

I trust the serendipity of inventive discovery, finding beauty in the unexpected.

I am a magnet for inspiration, attracting inventive ideas effortlessly and naturally.

I am a conduit for the universal flow of creative energy, channeling inspiration into my endeavors.

The tapestry of my thoughts is woven with threads of imaginative brilliance and ingenuity.

I release any fear of judgment and allow my creative expressions to flow authentically.

I am a vessel for the magic of inventive inspiration, and it flows through me effortlessly.

Challenges are opportunities for my inventive nature to shine.

The playground of my thoughts is a breeding ground for originality and creativity.

I welcome the unfolding of my imaginative potential in every moment.

Challenges are stepping stones, guiding me toward ingenious breakthroughs.

The tapestry of my ideas weaves together a rich mosaic of inventive possibilities.

I trust in the spontaneous dance of my thoughts, leading to innovative insights.

I trust the process of creative evolution, embracing each stage with openness and curiosity.

I am a conduit for the universal flow of creative energy, channeling inspiration into my endeavors.

The tapestry of my thoughts is woven with threads of imaginative brilliance and ingenuity.

I release any fear of judgment and allow my creative expressions to flow authentically.

I am a vessel for the magic of inventive inspiration, and it flows through me effortlessly.

My creative spirit is resilient, overcoming challenges with inventive solutions.

Every moment is an opportunity for creative expression and artistic exploration.

I am an architect of inventive ideas, constructing a reality that reflects my imaginative vision.

My mind is a fertile ground where ideas germinate, grow, and blossom into innovative concepts.

I trust the process of creative evolution, embracing each stage with openness and curiosity.

I embrace the beauty of uncertainty, knowing it often leads to profound moments of inspiration.

My mind is a sanctuary for innovative thoughts, where ideas bloom and flourish.

I welcome the flow of inventive energy, allowing it to inspire and uplift me.

I am open to creative breakthroughs that lead to new and exciting possibilities.

Challenges are invitations to tap into the well of inventive inspiration within me.

Every idea I conceive is a spark that ignites the flame of innovation within my soul.

My creative essence is resilient, overcoming challenges with inventive solutions.

Every moment is an opportunity for creative expression and artistic exploration.

I am an architect of inventive ideas, constructing a reality that reflects my imaginative vision.

My mind is a fertile ground where ideas germinate, grow, and blossom into innovative concepts.

The symphony of my inventive mind resonates with the harmonious frequencies of creativity.

I release any resistance to change, embracing inspiration that guides me to brilliance.

I am open to receiving inventive insights from unexpected sources and unlikely places.

The river of creative energy flows through me, carrying with it the seeds of new ideas.

Challenges serve as invitations to explore uncharted realms of inventive thinking.

Every idea I conceive is a stepping stone toward greater creativity and innovation.

My mind is a fertile ground for creative seeds to take root and flourish.

I trust the intuitive whispers of inventive inspiration that guide me toward inspired actions.

Challenges are opportunities for creative exploration and ingenious problem-solving.

The canvas of my life is painted with strokes of inventive brilliance and originality.

My thoughts are seeds of potential, germinating into lush forests of inventive concepts.

My mind is a wellspring of creative ideas and innovative solutions.

I effortlessly tap into my creative reservoir to generate inventive concepts.

Every challenge is an opportunity for my inventive nature to shine.

The playground of my thoughts is a breeding ground for originality and creativity.

I welcome the unfolding of my imaginative potential in every moment.

Challenges are stepping stones, guiding me toward ingenious breakthroughs.

The tapestry of my ideas weaves together a rich mosaic of inventive possibilities.

I trust in the spontaneous dance of my thoughts, leading to innovative insights.

My creative essence is a guiding force, fueling my journey towards new horizons.

The symphony of creativity resonates within me, guiding me towards inventive and ingenious solutions.

I welcome the unknown with excitement, trusting that creativity will illuminate the path ahead.

Every challenge is an opportunity for innovative problem-solving and creative growth.

I celebrate the dance of ideas in my mind, a choreography of inventive thoughts.

The wellspring of inventive energy within me is eternal, continually refreshing with new and imaginative ideas.

I trust in the infinite intelligence of my inventive mind, guiding me towards unique expressions.

I am an artist of thoughts, sculpting ideas into tangible and impactful forms.

The canvas of my mind is painted with strokes of inventive brilliance, creating a vibrant masterpiece.

I welcome the chaos of creative exploration, knowing that within it lies the seeds of innovation.

My thoughts are seeds of potential, germinating into lush forests of inventive concepts.

I release any fear of judgment, allowing my inventive expressions to shine authentically.

I am a vessel for the universal flow of inventive energy, shaping my reality with flair.

My mind is an open channel, inviting winds of inspiration to carry in new and novel concepts.

I embrace the cyclical nature of creativity, honoring periods of rest and reflection.

Challenges are mere stepping stones to innovative solutions and creative evolution.

The architecture of my thoughts is built with the bricks of inventive ideas and original designs.

I celebrate the kaleidoscope of ideas, recognizing each as a valuable contribution to my creativity.

My mind is a workshop where thoughts are sculpted into tangible expressions of ingenuity.

Every creative endeavor is a collaboration between my thoughts and the universal flow of inspiration.

I trust in the synchronicity of my inventive thoughts, leading me towards inspired actions.

I am an artist of thoughts, sculpting ideas into tangible and impactful forms.

The canvas of my mind is painted with strokes of inventive brilliance, creating a vibrant masterpiece.

I welcome the chaos of creative exploration, knowing that within it lies the seeds of innovation.

The essence of my thoughts is transformative, shaping my surroundings with inventive energy.

In my mental workshop, ideas are crafted into tangible expressions of ingenuity.

The symphony of my thoughts plays melodies that reverberate with inventive inspiration.

I am a conductor of innovative ideas, orchestrating a harmonious flow in my mind.

I welcome the dynamic interplay of ideas, blending them into a mosaic of creativity.

Every idea is a brushstroke painting the canvas of my mind with vibrant and imaginative hues.

I trust that the universe supports and amplifies my creative thought processes.

The symphony of creativity orchestrates beautiful melodies in every area of my life.

I release any fear of judgment, allowing my inventive expressions to radiate with authenticity.

I am a vessel for the universal flow of inventive energy, shaping my reality with flair.

My mind is a boundless canvas, ready to capture the brushstrokes of inspired thoughts.

I release any self-imposed limitations, allowing my inventive thoughts to soar to new heights.

The river of inspiration flows through me, carving new pathways and shaping my destiny.

Every creative endeavor is a tapestry woven with threads of innovation and ingenuity.

I celebrate the dance of ideas in my mind, a choreography of inventive thoughts.

The wellspring of inventive energy within me is eternal, continually refreshing with new and imaginative ideas.

I trust in the infinite intelligence of my inventive mind, guiding me toward unique expressions.

The symphony of my thoughts creates a melody of inspiration that echoes in my actions.

Challenges are gateways to creative solutions, and I navigate them with inventive flair.

The landscapes of my imagination continually evolve, offering new realms for exploration.

I release any limitations, allowing my thoughts to soar into innovative heights.

I celebrate the spontaneous dance of ideas in my mind, a ballet of inventiveness.

The river of inspiration flows gracefully through me, carving pathways of creative expression.

Every challenge is an opportunity to showcase my inventive and resourceful nature.

I trust in the serendipity of creative discovery, finding beauty in the unexpected.

I trust the serendipity of inventive discovery, finding beauty in the unexpected.

I am a magnet for inspiration, attracting inventive ideas effortlessly and naturally.

I am a magnet for inspiration, attracting inventive ideas effortlessly and naturally.

The symphony of creativity orchestrates beautiful melodies in every area of my life.

I release any fear of judgment, allowing my inventive expressions to radiate with authenticity.

I am a vessel for the universal flow of inventive energy, shaping my reality with flair.

My mind is a boundless canvas, ready to capture the brushstrokes of inspired thoughts.

I release any self-imposed limitations, allowing my inventive thoughts to soar to new heights.

The river of inspiration flows through me, carving new pathways and shaping my destiny.

Every creative endeavor is a tapestry woven with threads of innovation and ingenuity.

I celebrate the dance of ideas in my mind, a choreography of inventive thoughts.

The wellspring of inventive energy within me is eternal, continually refreshing with new and imaginative ideas.

I release any resistance to change, embracing inspiration that guides me to brilliance.

I am open to receiving inventive insights from unexpected sources and unlikely places.

The river of creative energy flows through me, carrying with it the seeds of new ideas.

Challenges serve as invitations to explore uncharted realms of inventive thinking.

Every idea I conceive is a stepping stone toward greater creativity and innovation.

My mind is a fertile ground for creative seeds to take root and flourish.

The canvas of my mind is painted with strokes of inventive brilliance, creating a vibrant masterpiece.

I welcome the chaos of creative exploration, knowing that within it lies the seeds of innovation.

My thoughts are seeds of potential, germinating into lush forests of inventive concepts.

I trust the serendipity of inventive discovery, finding beauty in the unexpected.

Every obstacle is a stepping stone toward unlocking fresh and inventive solutions.

I trust in the dynamic nature of my thoughts, adapting and evolving with creativity.

My mind is an expansive playground where ideas frolic and intertwine.

The landscapes of my imagination are ever-expanding, offering new vistas for exploration.

I trust in the divine flow of creative energy, allowing inspiration to guide my actions.

Every idea is a spark that ignites the flame of innovation within me.

I am a vessel for creative energy, allowing it to flow through me and manifest in beautiful ways.

I celebrate the diversity of my creative expressions, recognizing each as a unique masterpiece.

My mind is a fertile ground for creative seeds to take root and flourish.

I trust the intuitive whispers of inspiration that guide me towards inspired actions.

I celebrate the diversity of my creative expressions, recognizing each as a valuable contribution.

My mind is a workshop of endless possibilities, crafting ideas into tangible expressions.

Every creative endeavor is a collaboration between my thoughts and the universal flow of inspiration.

I embrace the serendipity of creative discovery, finding beauty in the unexpected.

I celebrate the spontaneous dance of inspiration, leading me to groundbreaking discoveries.

Every moment is an opportunity for a fresh and ingenious concept.

My thoughts are a symphony of originality, creating harmonies that resonate with the universe.

Challenges are gateways to inventive problem-solving and creative growth.

I welcome the diversity of thoughts, fostering a rich tapestry of imaginative expressions.

The canvas of my mind is painted with strokes of ingenious brilliance.

I trust the ebb and flow of my creative energy, allowing it to adapt and evolve effortlessly.

In the sanctuary of my mind, creative sparks illuminate the darkness, revealing endless possibilities.

The symphony of my thoughts plays a melody of innovation that reverberates through my actions.

I release any fear of judgment, allowing my creative expressions to flow authentically.

I am a vessel for the universal energy of inspiration, channeling it into my creative pursuits.

My thoughts are like seeds planted in the soil of my mind, growing into flourishing fields of creativity.

The architecture of my mind is built with the bricks of inventive ideas and imaginative designs.

I trust that the universe supports and amplifies my creative endeavors.

I am a conductor orchestrating the harmonious melodies of creative thoughts and ideas.

The currents of creative energy flow through me, connecting me to the infinite reservoir of inspiration.

The kaleidoscope of ideas in my mind forms a rich mosaic of creative possibilities.

The symphony of inspiration orchestrates beautiful melodies in every area of my life.

I welcome the unexpected twists and turns of my creative path, trusting they lead to new opportunities.

Challenges are mere gateways to innovative solutions, and I navigate through them with ease.

The fertile ground of my thoughts nurtures seeds of creativity that blossom into unique expressions.

Challenges are mere stepping stones, guiding me towards unexplored realms of inventive solutions.

Every idea is a journey, and I embark on these creative adventures with enthusiasm and curiosity.

The landscapes of my imagination are ever-expanding, offering new vistas for exploration.

The alchemy of my mind transforms ordinary thoughts into extraordinary and innovative concepts.

My creative intuition is a guiding star, leading me towards uncharted territories of inspiration.

My mind is an open channel, inviting winds of inspiration to carry in new and novel concepts.

I embrace the cyclical nature of inventiveness, honoring periods of rest and reflection.

Challenges are opportunities for inventive problem-solving and creative evolution.

The architecture of my thoughts is built with the bricks of inventive ideas and original designs.

My mind is an open gateway for inspiration, inviting inventive ideas to flow freely.

The seeds of innovation planted in my thoughts germinate into flourishing fields of creativity.

I celebrate the dance of ideas in my mind, a choreography of inventive concepts.

The river of inspiration flows gracefully through me, carving new pathways and shaping my destiny.

Challenges are mere stepping stones, guiding me towards innovative solutions and growth.

I trust the serendipity of inventive discovery, finding beauty in the unexpected.

Every obstacle is an opportunity for my inventive nature to showcase resilience and resourcefulness.

The symphony of creativity orchestrates beautiful melodies in every area of my life.

I release any fear of judgment, allowing my inventive expressions to radiate with authenticity.

I am a vessel for the universal flow of inventive energy, shaping my reality with flair.

My mind is a fertile ground where seeds of innovation sprout into groundbreaking concepts.

I embrace the dance of creativity, letting it guide me to new and unexplored territories.

Innovative solutions reveal themselves effortlessly, like stars illuminating the night sky.

Challenges are invitations for my inventive spirit to shine brightly and find ingenious answers.

Every thought carries the potential to birth a novel idea, contributing to the tapestry of innovation.

The symphony of my thoughts resonates with the harmonious chords of originality.

I am a conduit for inventive energy, channeling it into every aspect of my life.

The landscape of my mind is an ever-evolving canvas painted with strokes of ingenious ideas.

In the playground of my imagination, I joyfully explore the infinite realms of inventiveness.

I welcome the unpredictable nature of creative exploration, finding joy in the unexpected.

The canvas of my mind is painted with strokes of inventive brilliance, creating a vibrant masterpiece.

I welcome the chaos of creative exploration, knowing that within it lies the seeds of innovation.

My thoughts are seeds of potential, germinating into lush forests of inventive concepts.

I trust the serendipity of inventive discovery, finding beauty in the unexpected.

I am a magnet for inspiration, attracting inventive ideas effortlessly and naturally.

The symphony of creativity orchestrates beautiful melodies in every area of my life.

I release any fear of judgment, allowing my inventive expressions to radiate with authenticity.

I am a vessel for the universal flow of inventive energy, shaping my reality with flair.

My mind is a boundless canvas, ready to capture the brushstrokes of inspired thoughts.

The fountain of inventive ideas within me is boundless and ever-flowing.

I trust the serendipity of inventive discovery, finding beauty in the unexpected.

I am a magnet for inspiration, attracting inventive ideas effortlessly and naturally.

The symphony of creativity orchestrates beautiful melodies in every area of my life.

I release any fear of judgment, allowing my inventive expressions to radiate with authenticity.

I am a vessel for the universal flow of inventive energy, shaping my reality with flair.

Every creative endeavor is a tapestry woven with threads of innovation and ingenuity.

I celebrate the dance of ideas in my mind, a choreography of inventive thoughts.

The wellspring of inventive energy within me is eternal, continually refreshing with new and imaginative ideas.

I trust in the infinite intelligence of my inventive mind, guiding me towards unique expressions.

I am an artist of thoughts, sculpting ideas into tangible and impactful forms.

I release any self-imposed limitations, allowing my inventive thoughts to soar to new heights.

The river of inspiration flows through me, carving new pathways and shaping my destiny.

Every creative endeavor is a tapestry woven with threads of innovation and ingenuity.

I celebrate the dance of ideas in my mind, a choreography of inventive thoughts.

The wellspring of inventive energy within me is eternal, continually refreshing with new and imaginative ideas.

I trust in the infinite intelligence of my inventive mind, guiding me towards unique expressions.

I am an artist of thoughts, sculpting ideas into tangible and impactful forms.

The canvas of my mind is painted with strokes of inventive brilliance, creating a vibrant masterpiece.

I welcome the chaos of creative exploration, knowing that within it lies the seeds of innovation.

My thoughts are seeds of potential, germinating into lush forests of inventive concepts.

I release any self-imposed limitations, allowing my inventive thoughts to soar to new heights.

The river of inspiration flows through me, carving new pathways and shaping my destiny.

Every creative endeavor is a tapestry woven with threads of innovation and ingenuity.

I celebrate the dance of ideas in my mind, a choreography of inventive thoughts.

The wellspring of inventive energy within me is eternal, continually refreshing with new and imaginative ideas.

I trust in the infinite intelligence of my inventive mind, guiding me towards unique expressions.

I am an artist of thoughts, sculpting ideas into tangible and impactful forms.

The canvas of my mind is painted with strokes of inventive brilliance, creating a vibrant masterpiece.

I welcome the chaos of creative exploration, knowing that within it lies the seeds of innovation.

My thoughts are seeds of potential, germinating into lush forests of inventive concepts.

I am an artist of thoughts, sculpting ideas into tangible and impactful forms.

The canvas of my mind is painted with strokes of inventive brilliance, creating a vibrant masterpiece.

I welcome the chaos of creative exploration, knowing that within it lies the seeds of innovation.

My thoughts are seeds of potential, germinating into lush forests of inventive concepts.

I trust the serendipity of inventive discovery, finding beauty in the unexpected.

I am a magnet for inspiration, attracting inventive ideas effortlessly and naturally.

The symphony of creativity orchestrates beautiful melodies in every area of my life.

I release any fear of judgment, allowing my inventive expressions to radiate with authenticity.

I am a vessel for the universal flow of inventive energy, shaping my reality with flair.

My mind is a boundless canvas, ready to capture the brushstrokes of inspired thoughts.

The symphony of creativity orchestrates beautiful melodies in every area of my life.

I release any fear of judgment, allowing my inventive expressions to radiate with authenticity.

I am a vessel for the universal flow of inventive energy, shaping my reality with flair.

My mind is a boundless canvas, ready to capture the brushstrokes of inspired thoughts.

I release any self-imposed limitations, allowing my inventive thoughts to soar to new heights.

The river of inspiration flows through me, carving new pathways and shaping my destiny.

Every creative endeavor is a tapestry woven with threads of innovation and ingenuity.

I celebrate the dance of ideas in my mind, a choreography of inventive thoughts.

The wellspring of inventive energy within me is eternal, continually refreshing with new and imaginative ideas.

I trust in the infinite intelligence of my inventive mind, guiding me towards unique expressions.

My creative essence is a guiding force, fueling my journey towards new horizons.

I trust the serendipity of inventive discovery, finding beauty in the unexpected.

I am a magnet for inspiration, attracting inventive ideas effortlessly and naturally.

The symphony of creativity orchestrates beautiful melodies in every area of my life.

I release any fear of judgment, allowing my inventive expressions to radiate with authenticity.

I am a vessel for the universal flow of inventive energy, shaping my reality with flair.

My mind is a boundless canvas, ready to capture the brushstrokes of inspired thoughts.

I release any self-imposed limitations, allowing my inventive thoughts to soar to new heights.

I trust the serendipity of inventive discovery, finding beauty in the unexpected.

I am a magnet for inspiration, attracting inventive ideas effortlessly and naturally.

I am a conduit for the universal flow of creative energy, channeling inspiration into my endeavors.

The tapestry of my thoughts is woven with threads of imaginative brilliance and ingenuity.

I release any fear of judgment and allow my creative expressions to flow authentically.

I am a vessel for the magic of inventive inspiration, and it flows through me effortlessly.

Challenges are opportunities for my inventive nature to shine.

The playground of my thoughts is a breeding ground for originality and creativity.

I welcome the unfolding of my imaginative potential in every moment.

Challenges are stepping stones, guiding me toward ingenious breakthroughs.

The tapestry of my ideas weaves together a rich mosaic of inventive possibilities.

I trust in the spontaneous dance of my thoughts, leading to innovative insights.

I trust the process of creative evolution, embracing each stage with openness and curiosity.

I am a conduit for the universal flow of creative energy, channeling inspiration into my endeavors.

The tapestry of my thoughts is woven with threads of imaginative brilliance and ingenuity.

I release any fear of judgment and allow my creative expressions to flow authentically.

I am a vessel for the magic of inventive inspiration, and it flows through me effortlessly.

My creative spirit is resilient, overcoming challenges with inventive solutions.

Every moment is an opportunity for creative expression and artistic exploration.

I am an architect of inventive ideas, constructing a reality that reflects my imaginative vision.

My mind is a fertile ground where ideas germinate, grow, and blossom into innovative concepts.

I trust the process of creative evolution, embracing each stage with openness and curiosity.

I embrace the beauty of uncertainty, knowing it often leads to profound moments of inspiration.

My mind is a sanctuary for innovative thoughts, where ideas bloom and flourish.

I welcome the flow of inventive energy, allowing it to inspire and uplift me.

I am open to creative breakthroughs that lead to new and exciting possibilities.

Challenges are invitations to tap into the well of inventive inspiration within me.

Every idea I conceive is a spark that ignites the flame of innovation within my soul.

My creative essence is resilient, overcoming challenges with inventive solutions.

Every moment is an opportunity for creative expression and artistic exploration.

I am an architect of inventive ideas, constructing a reality that reflects my imaginative vision.

My mind is a fertile ground where ideas germinate, grow, and blossom into innovative concepts.

The symphony of my inventive mind resonates with the harmonious frequencies of creativity.

I release any resistance to change, embracing inspiration that guides me to brilliance.

I am open to receiving inventive insights from unexpected sources and unlikely places.

The river of creative energy flows through me, carrying with it the seeds of new ideas.

Challenges serve as invitations to explore uncharted realms of inventive thinking.

Every idea I conceive is a stepping stone toward greater creativity and innovation.

My mind is a fertile ground for creative seeds to take root and flourish.

I trust the intuitive whispers of inventive inspiration that guide me toward inspired actions.

Challenges are opportunities for creative exploration and ingenious problem-solving.

The canvas of my life is painted with strokes of inventive brilliance and originality.

My thoughts are seeds of potential, germinating into lush forests of inventive concepts.

My mind is a wellspring of creative ideas and innovative solutions.

I effortlessly tap into my creative reservoir to generate inventive concepts.

Every challenge is an opportunity for my inventive nature to shine.

The playground of my thoughts is a breeding ground for originality and creativity.

I welcome the unfolding of my imaginative potential in every moment.

Challenges are stepping stones, guiding me toward ingenious breakthroughs.

The tapestry of my ideas weaves together a rich mosaic of inventive possibilities.

I trust in the spontaneous dance of my thoughts, leading to innovative insights.

My creative essence is a guiding force, fueling my journey towards new horizons.

The symphony of creativity resonates within me, guiding me towards inventive and ingenious solutions.

I welcome the unknown with excitement, trusting that creativity will illuminate the path ahead.

Every challenge is an opportunity for innovative problem-solving and creative growth.

I celebrate the dance of ideas in my mind, a choreography of inventive thoughts.

The wellspring of inventive energy within me is eternal, continually refreshing with new and imaginative ideas.

I trust in the infinite intelligence of my inventive mind, guiding me towards unique expressions.

I am an artist of thoughts, sculpting ideas into tangible and impactful forms.

The canvas of my mind is painted with strokes of inventive brilliance, creating a vibrant masterpiece.

I welcome the chaos of creative exploration, knowing that within it lies the seeds of innovation.

My thoughts are seeds of potential, germinating into lush forests of inventive concepts.

I release any fear of judgment, allowing my inventive expressions to shine authentically.

I am a vessel for the universal flow of inventive energy, shaping my reality with flair.

My mind is an open channel, inviting winds of inspiration to carry in new and novel concepts.

I embrace the cyclical nature of creativity, honoring periods of rest and reflection.

Challenges are mere stepping stones to innovative solutions and creative evolution.

The architecture of my thoughts is built with the bricks of inventive ideas and original designs.

I celebrate the kaleidoscope of ideas, recognizing each as a valuable contribution to my creativity.

My mind is a workshop where thoughts are sculpted into tangible expressions of ingenuity.

Every creative endeavor is a collaboration between my thoughts and the universal flow of inspiration.

I trust in the synchronicity of my inventive thoughts, leading me towards inspired actions.

I am an artist of thoughts, sculpting ideas into tangible and impactful forms.

The canvas of my mind is painted with strokes of inventive brilliance, creating a vibrant masterpiece.

I welcome the chaos of creative exploration, knowing that within it lies the seeds of innovation.

The essence of my thoughts is transformative, shaping my surroundings with inventive energy.

In my mental workshop, ideas are crafted into tangible expressions of ingenuity.

The symphony of my thoughts plays melodies that reverberate with inventive inspiration.

I am a conductor of innovative ideas, orchestrating a harmonious flow in my mind.

I welcome the dynamic interplay of ideas, blending them into a mosaic of creativity.

Every idea is a brushstroke painting the canvas of my mind with vibrant and imaginative hues.

I trust that the universe supports and amplifies my creative thought processes.

The symphony of creativity orchestrates beautiful melodies in every area of my life.

I release any fear of judgment, allowing my inventive expressions to radiate with authenticity.

I am a vessel for the universal flow of inventive energy, shaping my reality with flair.

My mind is a boundless canvas, ready to capture the brushstrokes of inspired thoughts.

I release any self-imposed limitations, allowing my inventive thoughts to soar to new heights.

The river of inspiration flows through me, carving new pathways and shaping my destiny.

Every creative endeavor is a tapestry woven with threads of innovation and ingenuity.

I celebrate the dance of ideas in my mind, a choreography of inventive thoughts.

The wellspring of inventive energy within me is eternal, continually refreshing with new and imaginative ideas.

I trust in the infinite intelligence of my inventive mind, guiding me toward unique expressions.

The symphony of my thoughts creates a melody of inspiration that echoes in my actions.

Challenges are gateways to creative solutions, and I navigate them with inventive flair.

The landscapes of my imagination continually evolve, offering new realms for exploration.

I release any limitations, allowing my thoughts to soar into innovative heights.

I celebrate the spontaneous dance of ideas in my mind, a ballet of inventiveness.

The river of inspiration flows gracefully through me, carving pathways of creative expression.

Every challenge is an opportunity to showcase my inventive and resourceful nature.

I trust in the serendipity of creative discovery, finding beauty in the unexpected.

I trust the serendipity of inventive discovery, finding beauty in the unexpected.

I am a magnet for inspiration, attracting inventive ideas effortlessly and naturally.

I am a magnet for inspiration, attracting inventive ideas effortlessly and naturally.

The symphony of creativity orchestrates beautiful melodies in every area of my life.

I release any fear of judgment, allowing my inventive expressions to radiate with authenticity.

I am a vessel for the universal flow of inventive energy, shaping my reality with flair.

My mind is a boundless canvas, ready to capture the brushstrokes of inspired thoughts.

I release any self-imposed limitations, allowing my inventive thoughts to soar to new heights.

The river of inspiration flows through me, carving new pathways and shaping my destiny.

Every creative endeavor is a tapestry woven with threads of innovation and ingenuity.

I celebrate the dance of ideas in my mind, a choreography of inventive thoughts.

The wellspring of inventive energy within me is eternal, continually refreshing with new and imaginative ideas.

I release any resistance to change, embracing inspiration that guides me to brilliance.

I am open to receiving inventive insights from unexpected sources and unlikely places.

The river of creative energy flows through me, carrying with it the seeds of new ideas.

Challenges serve as invitations to explore uncharted realms of inventive thinking.

Every idea I conceive is a stepping stone toward greater creativity and innovation.

My mind is a fertile ground for creative seeds to take root and flourish.

The canvas of my mind is painted with strokes of inventive brilliance, creating a vibrant masterpiece.

I welcome the chaos of creative exploration, knowing that within it lies the seeds of innovation.

My thoughts are seeds of potential, germinating into lush forests of inventive concepts.

I trust the serendipity of inventive discovery, finding beauty in the unexpected.

Every obstacle is a stepping stone toward unlocking fresh and inventive solutions.

I trust in the dynamic nature of my thoughts, adapting and evolving with creativity.

My mind is an expansive playground where ideas frolic and intertwine.

The landscapes of my imagination are ever-expanding, offering new vistas for exploration.

I trust in the divine flow of creative energy, allowing inspiration to guide my actions.

Every idea is a spark that ignites the flame of innovation within me.

I am a vessel for creative energy, allowing it to flow through me and manifest in beautiful ways.

I celebrate the diversity of my creative expressions, recognizing each as a unique masterpiece.

My mind is a fertile ground for creative seeds to take root and flourish.

I trust the intuitive whispers of inspiration that guide me towards inspired actions.

I celebrate the diversity of my creative expressions, recognizing each as a valuable contribution.

My mind is a workshop of endless possibilities, crafting ideas into tangible expressions.

Every creative endeavor is a collaboration between my thoughts and the universal flow of inspiration.

I embrace the serendipity of creative discovery, finding beauty in the unexpected.

I celebrate the spontaneous dance of inspiration, leading me to groundbreaking discoveries.

Every moment is an opportunity for a fresh and ingenious concept.

My thoughts are a symphony of originality, creating harmonies that resonate with the universe.

Challenges are gateways to inventive problem-solving and creative growth.

I welcome the diversity of thoughts, fostering a rich tapestry of imaginative expressions.

The canvas of my mind is painted with strokes of ingenious brilliance.

I trust the ebb and flow of my creative energy, allowing it to adapt and evolve effortlessly.

In the sanctuary of my mind, creative sparks illuminate the darkness, revealing endless possibilities.

The symphony of my thoughts plays a melody of innovation that reverberates through my actions.

I release any fear of judgment, allowing my creative expressions to flow authentically.

I am a vessel for the universal energy of inspiration, channeling it into my creative pursuits.

My thoughts are like seeds planted in the soil of my mind, growing into flourishing fields of creativity.

The architecture of my mind is built with the bricks of inventive ideas and imaginative designs.

I trust that the universe supports and amplifies my creative endeavors.

I am a conductor orchestrating the harmonious melodies of creative thoughts and ideas.

The currents of creative energy flow through me, connecting me to the infinite reservoir of inspiration.

The kaleidoscope of ideas in my mind forms a rich mosaic of creative possibilities.

The symphony of inspiration orchestrates beautiful melodies in every area of my life.

I welcome the unexpected twists and turns of my creative path, trusting they lead to new opportunities.

Challenges are mere gateways to innovative solutions, and I navigate through them with ease.

The fertile ground of my thoughts nurtures seeds of creativity that blossom into unique expressions.

Challenges are mere stepping stones, guiding me towards unexplored realms of inventive solutions.

Every idea is a journey, and I embark on these creative adventures with enthusiasm and curiosity.

The landscapes of my imagination are ever-expanding, offering new vistas for exploration.

The alchemy of my mind transforms ordinary thoughts into extraordinary and innovative concepts.

My creative intuition is a guiding star, leading me towards uncharted territories of inspiration.

My mind is an open channel, inviting winds of inspiration to carry in new and novel concepts.

I embrace the cyclical nature of inventiveness, honoring periods of rest and reflection.

Challenges are opportunities for inventive problem-solving and creative evolution.

The architecture of my thoughts is built with the bricks of inventive ideas and original designs.

My mind is an open gateway for inspiration, inviting inventive ideas to flow freely.

The seeds of innovation planted in my thoughts germinate into flourishing fields of creativity.

I celebrate the dance of ideas in my mind, a choreography of inventive concepts.

The river of inspiration flows gracefully through me, carving new pathways and shaping my destiny.

Challenges are mere stepping stones, guiding me towards innovative solutions and growth.

I trust the serendipity of inventive discovery, finding beauty in the unexpected.

Every obstacle is an opportunity for my inventive nature to showcase resilience and resourcefulness.

The symphony of creativity orchestrates beautiful melodies in every area of my life.

I release any fear of judgment, allowing my inventive expressions to radiate with authenticity.

I am a vessel for the universal flow of inventive energy, shaping my reality with flair.

My mind is a fertile ground where seeds of innovation sprout into groundbreaking concepts.

I embrace the dance of creativity, letting it guide me to new and unexplored territories.

Innovative solutions reveal themselves effortlessly, like stars illuminating the night sky.

Challenges are invitations for my inventive spirit to shine brightly and find ingenious answers.

Every thought carries the potential to birth a novel idea, contributing to the tapestry of innovation.

The symphony of my thoughts resonates with the harmonious chords of originality.

I am a conduit for inventive energy, channeling it into every aspect of my life.

The landscape of my mind is an ever-evolving canvas painted with strokes of ingenious ideas.

In the playground of my imagination, I joyfully explore the infinite realms of inventiveness.

I welcome the unpredictable nature of creative exploration, finding joy in the unexpected.

The canvas of my mind is painted with strokes of inventive brilliance, creating a vibrant masterpiece.

I welcome the chaos of creative exploration, knowing that within it lies the seeds of innovation.

My thoughts are seeds of potential, germinating into lush forests of inventive concepts.

I trust the serendipity of inventive discovery, finding beauty in the unexpected.

I am a magnet for inspiration, attracting inventive ideas effortlessly and naturally.

The symphony of creativity orchestrates beautiful melodies in every area of my life.

I release any fear of judgment, allowing my inventive expressions to radiate with authenticity.

I am a vessel for the universal flow of inventive energy, shaping my reality with flair.

My mind is a boundless canvas, ready to capture the brushstrokes of inspired thoughts.

The fountain of inventive ideas within me is boundless and ever-flowing.

I trust the serendipity of inventive discovery, finding beauty in the unexpected.

I am a magnet for inspiration, attracting inventive ideas effortlessly and naturally.

The symphony of creativity orchestrates beautiful melodies in every area of my life.

I release any fear of judgment, allowing my inventive expressions to radiate with authenticity.

I am a vessel for the universal flow of inventive energy, shaping my reality with flair.

Every creative endeavor is a tapestry woven with threads of innovation and ingenuity.

I celebrate the dance of ideas in my mind, a choreography of inventive thoughts.

The wellspring of inventive energy within me is eternal, continually refreshing with new and imaginative ideas.

I trust in the infinite intelligence of my inventive mind, guiding me towards unique expressions.

I am an artist of thoughts, sculpting ideas into tangible and impactful forms.

I release any self-imposed limitations, allowing my inventive thoughts to soar to new heights.

The river of inspiration flows through me, carving new pathways and shaping my destiny.

Every creative endeavor is a tapestry woven with threads of innovation and ingenuity.

I celebrate the dance of ideas in my mind, a choreography of inventive thoughts.

The wellspring of inventive energy within me is eternal, continually refreshing with new and imaginative ideas.

I trust in the infinite intelligence of my inventive mind, guiding me towards unique expressions.

I am an artist of thoughts, sculpting ideas into tangible and impactful forms.

The canvas of my mind is painted with strokes of inventive brilliance, creating a vibrant masterpiece.

I welcome the chaos of creative exploration, knowing that within it lies the seeds of innovation.

My thoughts are seeds of potential, germinating into lush forests of inventive concepts.

I release any self-imposed limitations, allowing my inventive thoughts to soar to new heights.

The river of inspiration flows through me, carving new pathways and shaping my destiny.

Every creative endeavor is a tapestry woven with threads of innovation and ingenuity.

I celebrate the dance of ideas in my mind, a choreography of inventive thoughts.

The wellspring of inventive energy within me is eternal, continually refreshing with new and imaginative ideas.

I trust in the infinite intelligence of my inventive mind, guiding me towards unique expressions.

I am an artist of thoughts, sculpting ideas into tangible and impactful forms.

The canvas of my mind is painted with strokes of inventive brilliance, creating a vibrant masterpiece.

I welcome the chaos of creative exploration, knowing that within it lies the seeds of innovation.

My thoughts are seeds of potential, germinating into lush forests of inventive concepts.

I am an artist of thoughts, sculpting ideas into tangible and impactful forms.

The canvas of my mind is painted with strokes of inventive brilliance, creating a vibrant masterpiece.

I welcome the chaos of creative exploration, knowing that within it lies the seeds of innovation.

My thoughts are seeds of potential, germinating into lush forests of inventive concepts.

I trust the serendipity of inventive discovery, finding beauty in the unexpected.

I am a magnet for inspiration, attracting inventive ideas effortlessly and naturally.

The symphony of creativity orchestrates beautiful melodies in every area of my life.

I release any fear of judgment, allowing my inventive expressions to radiate with authenticity.

I am a vessel for the universal flow of inventive energy, shaping my reality with flair.

My mind is a boundless canvas, ready to capture the brushstrokes of inspired thoughts.

The symphony of creativity orchestrates beautiful melodies in every area of my life.

I release any fear of judgment, allowing my inventive expressions to radiate with authenticity.

I am a vessel for the universal flow of inventive energy, shaping my reality with flair.

My mind is a boundless canvas, ready to capture the brushstrokes of inspired thoughts.

I release any self-imposed limitations, allowing my inventive thoughts to soar to new heights.

The river of inspiration flows through me, carving new pathways and shaping my destiny.

Every creative endeavor is a tapestry woven with threads of innovation and ingenuity.

I celebrate the dance of ideas in my mind, a choreography of inventive thoughts.

The wellspring of inventive energy within me is eternal, continually refreshing with new and imaginative ideas.

I trust in the infinite intelligence of my inventive mind, guiding me towards unique expressions.

My creative essence is a guiding force, fueling my journey towards new horizons.

I trust the serendipity of inventive discovery, finding beauty in the unexpected.

I am a magnet for inspiration, attracting inventive ideas effortlessly and naturally.

The symphony of creativity orchestrates beautiful melodies in every area of my life.

I release any fear of judgment, allowing my inventive expressions to radiate with authenticity.

I am a vessel for the universal flow of inventive energy, shaping my reality with flair.

My mind is a boundless canvas, ready to capture the brushstrokes of inspired thoughts.

I release any self-imposed limitations, allowing my inventive thoughts to soar to new heights.

I trust the serendipity of inventive discovery, finding beauty in the unexpected.

I am a magnet for inspiration, attracting inventive ideas effortlessly and naturally.

I am a conduit for the universal flow of creative energy, channeling inspiration into my endeavors.

The tapestry of my thoughts is woven with threads of imaginative brilliance and ingenuity.

I release any fear of judgment and allow my creative expressions to flow authentically.

I am a vessel for the magic of inventive inspiration, and it flows through me effortlessly.

Challenges are opportunities for my inventive nature to shine.

The playground of my thoughts is a breeding ground for originality and creativity.

I welcome the unfolding of my imaginative potential in every moment.

Challenges are stepping stones, guiding me toward ingenious breakthroughs.

The tapestry of my ideas weaves together a rich mosaic of inventive possibilities.

I trust in the spontaneous dance of my thoughts, leading to innovative insights.

I trust the process of creative evolution, embracing each stage with openness and curiosity.

I am a conduit for the universal flow of creative energy, channeling inspiration into my endeavors.

The tapestry of my thoughts is woven with threads of imaginative brilliance and ingenuity.

I release any fear of judgment and allow my creative expressions to flow authentically.

I am a vessel for the magic of inventive inspiration, and it flows through me effortlessly.

My creative spirit is resilient, overcoming challenges with inventive solutions.

Every moment is an opportunity for creative expression and artistic exploration.

I am an architect of inventive ideas, constructing a reality that reflects my imaginative vision.

My mind is a fertile ground where ideas germinate, grow, and blossom into innovative concepts.

I trust the process of creative evolution, embracing each stage with openness and curiosity.

I embrace the beauty of uncertainty, knowing it often leads to profound moments of inspiration.

My mind is a sanctuary for innovative thoughts, where ideas bloom and flourish.

I welcome the flow of inventive energy, allowing it to inspire and uplift me.

I am open to creative breakthroughs that lead to new and exciting possibilities.

Challenges are invitations to tap into the well of inventive inspiration within me.

Every idea I conceive is a spark that ignites the flame of innovation within my soul.

My creative essence is resilient, overcoming challenges with inventive solutions.

Every moment is an opportunity for creative expression and artistic exploration.

I am an architect of inventive ideas, constructing a reality that reflects my imaginative vision.

My mind is a fertile ground where ideas germinate, grow, and blossom into innovative concepts.

The symphony of my inventive mind resonates with the harmonious frequencies of creativity.

I release any resistance to change, embracing inspiration that guides me to brilliance.

I am open to receiving inventive insights from unexpected sources and unlikely places.

The river of creative energy flows through me, carrying with it the seeds of new ideas.

Challenges serve as invitations to explore uncharted realms of inventive thinking.

Every idea I conceive is a stepping stone toward greater creativity and innovation.

My mind is a fertile ground for creative seeds to take root and flourish.

I trust the intuitive whispers of inventive inspiration that guide me toward inspired actions.

Challenges are opportunities for creative exploration and ingenious problem-solving.

The canvas of my life is painted with strokes of inventive brilliance and originality.

My thoughts are seeds of potential, germinating into lush forests of inventive concepts.

My mind is a wellspring of creative ideas and innovative solutions.

I effortlessly tap into my creative reservoir to generate inventive concepts.

Every challenge is an opportunity for my inventive nature to shine.

The playground of my thoughts is a breeding ground for originality and creativity.

I welcome the unfolding of my imaginative potential in every moment.

Challenges are stepping stones, guiding me toward ingenious breakthroughs.

The tapestry of my ideas weaves together a rich mosaic of inventive possibilities.

I trust in the spontaneous dance of my thoughts, leading to innovative insights.

My creative essence is a guiding force, fueling my journey towards new horizons.

The symphony of creativity resonates within me, guiding me towards inventive and ingenious solutions.

I welcome the unknown with excitement, trusting that creativity will illuminate the path ahead.

Every challenge is an opportunity for innovative problem-solving and creative growth.

I celebrate the dance of ideas in my mind, a choreography of inventive thoughts.

The wellspring of inventive energy within me is eternal, continually refreshing with new and imaginative ideas.

I trust in the infinite intelligence of my inventive mind, guiding me towards unique expressions.

I am an artist of thoughts, sculpting ideas into tangible and impactful forms.

The canvas of my mind is painted with strokes of inventive brilliance, creating a vibrant masterpiece.

I welcome the chaos of creative exploration, knowing that within it lies the seeds of innovation.

My thoughts are seeds of potential, germinating into lush forests of inventive concepts.

I release any fear of judgment, allowing my inventive expressions to shine authentically.

I am a vessel for the universal flow of inventive energy, shaping my reality with flair.

My mind is an open channel, inviting winds of inspiration to carry in new and novel concepts.

I embrace the cyclical nature of creativity, honoring periods of rest and reflection.

Challenges are mere stepping stones to innovative solutions and creative evolution.

The architecture of my thoughts is built with the bricks of inventive ideas and original designs.

I celebrate the kaleidoscope of ideas, recognizing each as a valuable contribution to my creativity.

My mind is a workshop where thoughts are sculpted into tangible expressions of ingenuity.

Every creative endeavor is a collaboration between my thoughts and the universal flow of inspiration.

I trust in the synchronicity of my inventive thoughts, leading me towards inspired actions.

I am an artist of thoughts, sculpting ideas into tangible and impactful forms.

The canvas of my mind is painted with strokes of inventive brilliance, creating a vibrant masterpiece.

I welcome the chaos of creative exploration, knowing that within it lies the seeds of innovation.

The essence of my thoughts is transformative, shaping my surroundings with inventive energy.

In my mental workshop, ideas are crafted into tangible expressions of ingenuity.

The symphony of my thoughts plays melodies that reverberate with inventive inspiration.

I am a conductor of innovative ideas, orchestrating a harmonious flow in my mind.

I welcome the dynamic interplay of ideas, blending them into a mosaic of creativity.

Every idea is a brushstroke painting the canvas of my mind with vibrant and imaginative hues.

I trust that the universe supports and amplifies my creative thought processes.

The symphony of creativity orchestrates beautiful melodies in every area of my life.

I release any fear of judgment, allowing my inventive expressions to radiate with authenticity.

I am a vessel for the universal flow of inventive energy, shaping my reality with flair.

My mind is a boundless canvas, ready to capture the brushstrokes of inspired thoughts.

I release any self-imposed limitations, allowing my inventive thoughts to soar to new heights.

The river of inspiration flows through me, carving new pathways and shaping my destiny.

Every creative endeavor is a tapestry woven with threads of innovation and ingenuity.

I celebrate the dance of ideas in my mind, a choreography of inventive thoughts.

The wellspring of inventive energy within me is eternal, continually refreshing with new and imaginative ideas.

I trust in the infinite intelligence of my inventive mind, guiding me toward unique expressions.

The symphony of my thoughts creates a melody of inspiration that echoes in my actions.

Challenges are gateways to creative solutions, and I navigate them with inventive flair.

The landscapes of my imagination continually evolve, offering new realms for exploration.

I release any limitations, allowing my thoughts to soar into innovative heights.

I celebrate the spontaneous dance of ideas in my mind, a ballet of inventiveness.

The river of inspiration flows gracefully through me, carving pathways of creative expression.

Every challenge is an opportunity to showcase my inventive and resourceful nature.

I trust in the serendipity of creative discovery, finding beauty in the unexpected.

I trust the serendipity of inventive discovery, finding beauty in the unexpected.

I am a magnet for inspiration, attracting inventive ideas effortlessly and naturally.

I am a magnet for inspiration, attracting inventive ideas effortlessly and naturally.

The symphony of creativity orchestrates beautiful melodies in every area of my life.

I release any fear of judgment, allowing my inventive expressions to radiate with authenticity.

I am a vessel for the universal flow of inventive energy, shaping my reality with flair.

My mind is a boundless canvas, ready to capture the brushstrokes of inspired thoughts.

I release any self-imposed limitations, allowing my inventive thoughts to soar to new heights.

The river of inspiration flows through me, carving new pathways and shaping my destiny.

Every creative endeavor is a tapestry woven with threads of innovation and ingenuity.

I celebrate the dance of ideas in my mind, a choreography of inventive thoughts.

The wellspring of inventive energy within me is eternal, continually refreshing with new and imaginative ideas.

I release any resistance to change, embracing inspiration that guides me to brilliance.

I am open to receiving inventive insights from unexpected sources and unlikely places.

The river of creative energy flows through me, carrying with it the seeds of new ideas.

Challenges serve as invitations to explore uncharted realms of inventive thinking.

Every idea I conceive is a stepping stone toward greater creativity and innovation.

My mind is a fertile ground for creative seeds to take root and flourish.

The canvas of my mind is painted with strokes of inventive brilliance, creating a vibrant masterpiece.

I welcome the chaos of creative exploration, knowing that within it lies the seeds of innovation.

My thoughts are seeds of potential, germinating into lush forests of inventive concepts.

I trust the serendipity of inventive discovery, finding beauty in the unexpected.

I celebrate the dance of ideas in my mind, a choreography
of inventive thoughts.

The wellspring of inventive energy within me is eternal,
continually refreshing with new and imaginative ideas.

I release any resistance to change, embracing inspiration
that guides me to brilliance.

I am open to receiving inventive insights from unexpected
sources and unlikely places.

The river of creative energy flows through me, carrying
with it the seeds of new ideas.

Challenges serve as invitations to explore uncharted realms
of inventive thinking.

Every idea I conceive is a stepping stone toward greater
creativity and innovation.

My mind is a fertile ground for creative seeds to take root
and flourish.

The canvas of my mind is painted with strokes of inventive
brilliance, creating a vibrant masterpiece.

I welcome the chaos of creative exploration, knowing that
within it lies the seeds of innovation.

My thoughts are seeds of potential, germinating into lush
forests of inventive concepts.

I trust the serendipity of inventive discovery, finding
beauty in the unexpected.